AP 6 '90			
MR 13 '92			
MY 15 '92			
DE2 0 '98			
NO 23 '98			
MY 20 '99			
MY 16 00			
MR 21 00			
JY 23 00			
AG 8 00			

DEMCO 38-297   JAN '90

Modern Critical Interpretations

William Shakespeare's
Twelfth Night

Modern Critical Interpretations

These and other titles in preparation

William Shakespeare's
Twelfth Night

Edited and with an introduction by

Harold Bloom
Sterling Professor of the Humanities
Yale University

Chelsea House Publishers ◊ *1987*

NEW YORK ◊ NEW HAVEN ◊ PHILADELPHIA

© 1987 by Chelsea House Publishers, a division
of Chelsea House Educational Communications, Inc.,
   95 Madison Avenue, New York, NY 10016
   345 Whitney Avenue, New Haven, CT 06511
   5014 West Chester Pike, Edgemont, PA 19028

Introduction © 1987 by Harold Bloom

Printed and bound in the United States of America

∞ The paper used in this publication meets the minimum
requirements of the American National Standard for Permanence
of Paper for Printed Library Materials, Z39.48-1984.

Library of Congress Cataloging-in-Publication Data
William Shakespeare's Twelfth night.
   (Modern critical interpretations)
   Includes index.
   Summary: A collection of ten critical essays on the
Shakespearan comedy, arranged in chronological order of
original publication.
   1. Shakespeare, William 1564–1616. Twelfth night.
[1. Shakespeare, William, 1564–1616. Twelfth night.
2. English literature—History and criticism]   I. Bloom,
Harold.   II. Series.
PR2837.W54   1987   822.3′3   87-5146
ISBN 0–87754–941–9 (alk. paper)

Contents

Editor's Note

This book gathers together a representative selection of what I judge to be the best modern criticism upon Shakespeare's *Twelfth Night*. The critical essays are reprinted here in the chronological order of their original publication. I am grateful to Kathryn Treadwell, Marena Fisher, and Susan Laity for their aid in editing this volume.

My introduction centers upon Feste and Malvolio, while attempting a description of the play that highlights its overt outrageousness. John Hollander, poet and scholarly critic of the idea of music throughout poetry, begins the chronological sequence with an analysis of the function of music as metaphor in *Twelfth Night*.

A Marxist reading by Elliot Krieger seeks to locate Malvolio's fate in the context of Elizabethan class distinctions, while conducting an argument against the views on *Twelfth Night* of Hollander and C. L. Barber. Ruth Nevo naturally concentrates on the ways in which Viola shows Olivia what a true man should be and shows Orsino what a true woman should be. In complements to that, Coppélia Kahn considers sexual experimentation in role playing and Karen Greif looks at other kinds of deception in the play. Camille Slights discusses the question of who gets what, monetarily and otherwise in *Twelfth Night*, while Elizabeth M. Yearling sets the drama in the context of Renaissance views of language.

In Jean E. Howard's essay, *Twelfth Night* is analyzed as a theatrical experience, while Gary Taylor considers how we apprehend Viola theatrically, both in terms of speech acts, and by contrasts with other characters. This book ends with an essay by Geoffrey H. Hartman, one of our most advanced critical theorists, who finds in *Twelfth Night* a partial portrait of what the eighteenth-century critics called Shakespeare's Poetical Character.

Introduction

Clearly a kind of farewell to unmixed comedy, *Twelfth Night* nevertheless seems to me much the funniest of Shakespeare's plays, though I have yet to see it staged in a way consonant with its full humor. As some critics have noted, only Feste the clown among all its characters is essentially sane, and even he allows himself to be dragged into the tormenting of the wretched Malvolio, whose only culpability is that he finds himself in the wrong play, as little at home there as Shylock is in Venice.

Everything about *Twelfth Night* is unsettling, except for Feste again, and even he might be happier in a different play. Perhaps *Twelfth Night* was Shakespeare's practical joke upon his audience, turning all of them into Malvolios. Like *Measure for Measure*, the play would be perfectly rancid if it took itself seriously, which it wisely refuses to do. *Twelfth Night*, I would suggest, is a highly deliberate outrage, and should be played as such. Except for Feste, yet once more, none of its characters ought to be portrayed wholly sympathetically, not even Viola, who is herself a kind of passive zany, since who else would fall in love with the self-intoxicated Orsino?

What is most outrageous about *Twelfth Night* is Shakespeare's deliberate self-parody, which mocks his own originality at representation and thus savages representation or aesthetic imitation itself. Nothing happens in *Twelfth Night*, so there is no action to imitate anyway; *The Tempest* at least represents its opening storm, but *Twelfth Night* shrugs off its own, as if to say perfunctorily: let's get started. The shrug is palpable enough when we first meet Viola, at the start of scene 2:

> VIOLA. What country, friends, is this?
> CAPTAIN. This is Illyria, lady.
> VIOLA. And what should I do in Illyria?
>   My brother he is in Elysium.
>   Perchance he is not drown'd—what think you, sailors?

1

Illyria is a kind of madcap Elysium, as we have discovered already, if we have listened intently to the superbly eloquent and quite crazy opening speech of its Duke:

> If music be the food of love, play on,
> Give me excess of it; that surfeiting,
> The appetite may sicken, and so die.
> That strain again, it had a dying fall;
> O, it came o'er my ear like the sweet sound
> That breathes upon a bank of violets,
> Stealing and giving odor. Enough, no more,
> 'Tis not so sweet now as it was before.
> O spirit of love, how quick and fresh art thou,
> That notwithstanding thy capacity
> Receiveth as the sea, nought enters there,
> Of what validity and pitch soe'er,
> But falls into abatement and low price
> Even in a minute. So full of shapes is fancy
> That it alone is high fantastical.

Shakespeare himself so liked Orsino's opening conceit that he returned to it five years later in *Antony and Cleopatra* where Cleopatra, missing Antony, commands: "Give me some music; music, moody food / Of us that trade in love." Orsino, not a trader in love but a glutton for the idea of it, is rather more like John Keats than he is like Cleopatra, and his beautiful opening speech is inevitably echoed in Keats's "Ode on Melancholy." We can call Orsino a Keats gone bad, or even a little mad, returning us again to the mad behavior of nearly everyone in *Twelfth Night*. Dr. Samuel Johnson, who feared madness, liked to attribute rational design even where it seems unlikely:

> Viola seems to have formed a very deep design with very little premeditation: she is thrown by shipwreck on an unknown coast, hears that the prince is a batchelor, and resolves to supplant the lady whom he courts.

Anne Barton more accurately gives us a very different Viola, whose "boy's disguise operates not as a liberation but merely as a way of going underground in a difficult situation." Even that seems to me rather more rational than the play's Viola, who never does come up from underground, but, then, except for Feste, who does? Feste surely speaks the play's only wisdom: "And thus the whirligig of time brings in his revenges." "Time is a child playing draughts; the lordship is to the child" is the dark wisdom of Heracleitus. Nietzsche, with some desperation, had his Zarathustra proclaim the will's revenge against time, and in particular against time's assertion, "It was." Shakespeare's time plays with a spinning top, so that time's revenges presumably have a circular aspect. Yet Feste sings that when he was a young fool, he was taken as a toy, certainly not the way we take him now. He knows what most critics of Shakespeare will not learn, which is that *Twelfth Night* does not come to any true resolution, in which anyone has learned anything. Malvolio might be an exemplary figure if we could smuggle him into a play by Ben Jonson, but *Twelfth Night*, as John Hollander long ago noted, appears to be a deliberately anti-Jonsonian drama. No one could or should be made better by viewing or reading it.

If it has no moral coherence, where then shall its coherence be found? Orsino, baffled by the first joint appearance of the twins Viola and Sebastian, is driven to a famous outburst:

> One face, one voice, one habit, and two persons,
> A natural perspective, that is and is not!

Anne Barton glosses this as an optical illusion naturally produced, rather than given by a distorting perspective glass. Dr. Johnson gives the same reading rather more severely: "that nature has here exhibited such a show, where shadows seem realities; where that which 'is not' appears like that which 'is.'" A natural perspective is in this sense oxymoronic, unless time and nature are taken as identical, so that time's whirligig then would become the same toy as the distorting glass. If we could imagine a distorting mirror whirling in circles like a top, we would have the compound toy that *Twelfth Night* constituted for Shakespeare. Reflections in that mirror are the representations in *Twelfth Night*: Viola, Olivia, Sir Toby and Sir Andrew, Orsino, Sebastian, and all the rest except for Malvolio and Feste.

It is difficult for me to see Malvolio as an anti–Puritan satire, because Sir Toby, Sir Andrew, and Maria are figures even more unattractive, by any imaginative standards. Sir Toby is not a Falstaffian personage, no matter what critics have said. Falstaff without preternatural wit is not Falstaff, and Belch is just that: belch, rather than cakes and ale. Malvolio is an instance of a character who gets away even from Shakespeare, another hobgoblin run off with the garland of Apollo, like Shylock or like both Angelo and Barnardine in *Measure for Measure*. The relations between Ben Jonson and Shakespeare must have been lively, complex, and mutually ambivalent, and Malvolio seems to me Shakespeare's slyest thrust at Jonsonian dramatic morality. But even as we laugh at Malvolio's fall, a laughter akin to the savage merriment doubtless provoked in the Elizabethan audience by the fall of Shylock, so we are made uneasy at the fate of Malvolio and Shylock alike. Something in us rightly shudders when we are confronted by the vision of poor Malvolio bound in the dark room. An uncanny cognitive music emerges in the dialogue between Feste, playing Sir Topas the curate, and "Malvolio the lunatic":

> MALVOLIO. Sir Topas, Sir Topas, good Sir Topas, go to my lady.
>
> CLOWN. Out, hyperbolical fiend! how vexest thou this man! Talkest thou nothing but of ladies?
>
> SIR TOBY. Well said, Master Parson.
>
> MALVOLIO. Sir Topas, never was man thus wrong'd. Good Sir Topas, do not think I am mad; they have laid me here in hideous darkness.
>
> CLOWN. Fie, thou dishonest Sathan! I call thee by the most modest terms, for I am one of those gentle ones that will use the devil himself with courtesy. Say'st thou that house is dark?
>
> MALVOLIO. As hell, Sir Topas.
>
> CLOWN. Why, it hath bay windows transparent as barricadoes, and the [clerestories] toward the south north are as lustrous as ebony; and yet complainest thou of obstruction?
>
> MALVOLIO. I am not mad, Sir Topas, I say to you this house is dark.
>
> CLOWN. Madman, thou errest. I say there is no darkness but ignorance, in which thou art more puzzled than the Egyptians in their fog.
>
> MALVOLIO. I say this house is as dark as ignorance, though ignorance were as dark as hell; and I say there was never man thus abus'd. I am no more mad than you are; make the trial of it in any constant question.
>
> CLOWN. What is the opinion of Pythagoras concerning wild-fowl?
>
> MALVOLIO. That the soul of our grandam might happily inhabit a bird.
>
> CLOWN. What think'st thou of his opinion?
>
> MALVOLIO. I think nobly of the soul, and no way approve his opinion.

CLOWN. Fare thee well. Remain thou still in darkness. Thou
  shalt hold th' opinion of Pythagoras ere I will allow of
  thy wits, and fear to kill a woodcock lest thou dispossess
  the soul of thy grandam. Fare thee well.
MALVOLIO. Sir Topas, Sir Topas!

We are almost in the cosmos of *King Lear*, in Lear's wild dialogues with
Edgar and Gloucester. Feste is sublimely wise, warning Malvolio against
the ignorance of his Jonsonian moral pugnacity, which can make one as
stupid as a woodcock. But there is a weirder cognitive warning in Feste's
Pythagorian wisdom. Metempsychosis or the instability of identity is the
essence of *Twelfth Night*, the lesson that none of its characters are capable of
learning, except for Feste, who learns it better all the time, even as the
whirligig of time brings in his revenges:

> A great while ago the world begun,
>   With hey ho, the wind and the rain,
> But that's all one, our play is done,
>   And we'll strive to please you every day.

Shakespeare's Many Sorts of Music

John Hollander

When seen in the light of the richness of sixteenth-century musical thought, the modern academic question of "Shakespeare and Music" tends to be more blinding than the glittering of its generality would warrant. With the aid of the musicological studies of the past thirty years, we are better able than ever before to reconstruct the actual music performed in and referred to in Shakespeare's plays. The growth of studies in the History of Ideas has given us models for understanding how words and customs that have mis-leadingly retained their forms to this day reverberated differently in various historical contexts. The forays of sixteenth- and seventeenth-century poets into *musica speculativa*, consequently, can now be understood as more than either the fanciful conceits or the transmission of quaint lore that many nineteenth-century readers took them to be. But the recent critical tradi-tions that read all of Shakespeare with the kind of attention previously devoted to other kinds of poetry have tended to create a third, queer cate-gory of symbolic music. G. Wilson Knight in particular has employed the images of tempest and music in his criticism to suggest the universal themes of disorder and resolving, reconciling order. These concepts stem largely from his invaluable early work on the last plays, in which, trivially speak-ing, storm and music do appear to alternate.

But Professor Wilson Knight's notion of Shakespearean "music" tends often to get out of hand. He confuses the actual practice of music on the Elizabethan and Jacobean stage with *musica speculativa* and musical imagery in the texts of the plays themselves, and both of these, finally, with his own

From *The Untuning of the Sky: Ideas of Music in English Poetry 1500–1700*. © 1961 by John Hollander. Princeton University Press, 1961.

notion of "music" as a critical term for a general condition of transcendent order. Thus he can say of music that "Shakespeare's use of it is very straight-forward. No author would give directions for soft music whilst Duncan is being murdered: the music-love associations in Shakespeare are as natural as his tempests."

The objections that might be raised are numerous here, but I shall content myself with observing that in the first place, Marston in *The Malcontent* seems to have done just what it is asserted that no author would do, and that in the second place, a dangerous mixture of categories occurs in the last clause. While tempests as plot devices (and their noises as sound effect and stage property) remain fairly regularized throughout Elizabethan and Jacobean drama, the use of music cannot be said to do so. Instead, a great change occurs when one moves from the outdoor theaters with their elaborate use of music in signalling functions and the necessity of incorporating all music except these signals into the plot of the play itself. The small coterie theaters of the city, with their more elaborate court and chapel musical connections, followed the masque eventually in developing a musical consort whose playing was more or less a *donnée*, and whose presence need not always be explained by a cry of "Ho, the recorders" or the like. It is perhaps the influence of the coterie theaters and their musical conventions which lead to the masque-like use of music in Shakespeare's late plays, and to what Professor Wilson Knight calls "the mysterious symbolic music that accompanies Antony's failure as a soldier and his dying into love."

It is essentially a romantic, if not actually a *symboliste* notion of music which Professor Wilson Knight employs, and aside from his naive treatment of sixteenth-century music and attitudes toward it, his insistence on Shakespeare's symbolic music ignores conventions of musical imagery and exegesis in Renaissance literature. Worse than this, however, has been the effect of his failure to see exactly to what degree Shakespeare's poetic intelligence utilized received ideas about music, both speculative and practical, analyzing and reinterpreting them in dramatic contexts. Finally, and perhaps worst of all, some of Shakespeare's amazingly original contributions to *musica speculativa* have been lost sight of.

Many of the musical subjects and images that appear in Shakespeare's plays and poems are of a more or less conventional quality. By and large, the bulk of the references in all the plays is to practical music, which is cited, satirized, and praised in various contexts like any other human activity. Of particular interest to Shakespeare always was the richness of various technical vocabularies, and much of the wit in all but the later plays consists of puns and twisted tropes on technical terminology, often that of instrumental music. Two well-known passages of *musica speculativa* in the earlier plays, however, deserve some comment.

The first of these is Richard II's great speech in Pomfret Castle. After likening his prison to the world and to his own body, the King hears music offstage:

> Music do I hear?
> Ha, ha! Keep time. How sour sweet music is
> When time is broke and no proportion kept!
> So is it in the music of men's lives,
> And here have I the daintiness of ear
> To check time broke in a disordered string,
> But for the concord of my state and time
> Had not an ear to hear my true time broke.
>
> (5.5.41–48)

"Proportion" here is used in its immediate sense of time-signature, and "Time broke in a disordered string" refers to the music he hears playing. But the "disordered string" is also himself, an emblem of the unruled, unruly state. "The concord of my state and time" invokes the musical connotations of "concord" as well—for centuries the world had reverberated with the old pun on "heart" and "string." What the King is saying is that now, in his broken state, he is sensitive to all the nuances of musical order, but formerly, lulled by the metaphorically musical order of his earlier reign, he had been unable to hear the tentative tempi in his own *musica humana*. In this passage an occurrence of practical music is interpreted in perfectly traditional terms, and human and worldly musics are made to coincide, both in Richard's own rhetoric and in the hierarchical imagery throughout the play. The conventional multiplicity of extensions of the term "music" are employed directly, and Richard, aside from the tireless progression of his thoughts, is talking like something out of an old book.

The final irony of Richard's soliloquy,

> This music mads me, let it sound no more,
> For though it have holp madmen to their wits,
> In me it seems it will make wise men mad.
> Yet blessings on his heart that gives it me!
> For 'tis a sign of love, and love to Richard
> Is a strange brooch in this all-hating world.
>
> (5.5.61–66)

is reinforced by the fragmentation of "music" into its various categories. The music is maddening because its human and universal roles have not coincided for the King, whose necessary identity with the proper order of the state has been called into question by the fact of his deposition and imprisonment. Bolingbroke, the discord, the untuner, has himself become the well-tuned, regulating instrument of state. And, finally, the practical music is sundered from its speculative form in Richard's gratitude for the instrumental sounds themselves, which he takes as the evidence of some-one's thoughtful care.

I believe that it is this same conventional use of the emblematic stringed instrument in a political context that is at work during a moment in Bru-tus's tent in act 4, scene 3, of *Julius Caesar*. The boy Lucius has fallen asleep over his instrument after singing for Brutus, and the latter has taken it away from him lest it drop to the ground and break. After the ominous ap-pearance of Caesar's ghost, Brutus cries out, and the boy half-awakens, murmuring, "The strings, my lord, are false." Brutus, missing the import of this, comments, "He thinks he still is at his instrument," and shakes Lucius fully awake, inquiring after the phantom. But the meaning, I think, is clear, and the false strings suggest the discordant conspirators, now jan-gling and out of tune even among themselves. Brutus, who "in general honest thought / And common good to all, made one" of the varying faction he led, meets the prophetic truth of the boy's half-dreamed image with a benevolently naturalistic interpretation of it.

The even better-known music at Belmont in *The Merchant of Venice* shows a more dramatically sophisticated use of *musica speculativa*. In general, the dramatic structure of the whole play hinges on the relationship between Venice, the commercial city where gold is ventured for more gold, and the symbolically golden Belmont, where all is hazarded for love. Belmont is full of practical music in one of its most common sixteenth-century forms. Music used for signalling, the tuckets, flourishes, and sennets familiar to modern readers through stage directions, were not confined to the uses of dramaturgy; it was a matter of actual practice for distinguished persons to be accompanied by their private trumpeters. It is almost as a signal that the song "Tell me where is fancy bred" is employed. Like a nursery-rhyme riddle, it advises against appearances, and cryptically urges the choice of the lead. In a speech preceding the song, Portia's wit analyzes and interprets the ceremonial music she has ordered:

> Let music sound while he doth make his choice,
> Then, if he lose, he makes a swanlike end,

Fading in music. That the comparison
May stand more proper, my eye shall be the stream
And watery deathbed for him. He may win,
And what is music then? Then music is
Even as the flourish when true subjects bow
To a new-crowned monarch.

(3.2.43–50)

Here Portia makes the point that the same music can play many roles, that the concept emerges from the fact as the result of an intellectual process. She selects two polar concepts, incidentally: music as signal, which plays little or no part in traditional musical speculation, and the myth of the dying swan, a stock image in romantic lyrics throughout the century. Portia reaffirms this later on, when she remarks of the music that Jessica and Lorenzo hear on the bank, "Nothing is good, I see, without respect. / Methinks it sounds much sweeter than by day." Nerissa replies that "Silence bestows that virtue on it," invoking one of the dominant Belmont themes of the deception of ornament, of the paleness more moving than eloquence. It is the same theme that prefaces Lorenzo's initiation of Jessica into the silent *harmonia mundi*:

Soft stillness and the night
Become the touches of sweet harmony.
Sit, Jessica. Look how the floor of heaven
Is thick inlaid with patines of bright gold.
There's not the smallest orb which thou behold'st
But in his motion like an angel sings,
Still quiring to the young-ey'd cherubins.
Souch harmony is in immortal souls,
But whilst this muddy vesture of decay
Doth grossly close it in, we cannot hear it.

(5.1.56–65)

This is the vision of Plato's Er and Cicero's Scipio. It is significant that the one instance of Shakespeare's troping of the doctrine is Lorenzo's explanation of the inaudible character of the heavenly music. Neither of the traditional reasons (acclimatization, or the physical thresholds of perception) is given. Instead, the unheard music is related to immortality, and by extension to a prelapsarian condition, a world which, like heaven, need not conceal its ultimate gold, which even Belmont must do. This approaches Milton's treatment of the subject in *At a Solemn Music*.

Then enter the musicians, to play at Lorenzo's bidding. "I am never merry when I hear sweet music," says Jessica, and here she uses "sweet" to mean "perfectly tuned" in the same standard sixteenth-century sense that was employed by Richard in Pomfret Castle. Renaissance musical doctrine would answer her question by reference to the gravity of the celestial harmony that is engaged by any truly tuned earthly musical proportions. Lorenzo retorts with a traditional disquisition on music and the affections, ending on a note of *musica humana* with all of its ethical and political connotations:

> The reason is, your spirits are attentive.
> For do but note a wild and wanton herd,
> Or race of youthful and unhandled colts,
> Fetching mad bounds, bellowing, and neighing loud,
> Which is the hot condition of their blood.
> If they but hear perchance a trumpet sound,
> Or any air of music touch their ears,
> You shall perceive them make a mutual stand,
> Their savage eyes turned to a modest gaze
> By the sweet power of music. Therefore the poet
> Did feign that Orpheus drew trees, stones, and floods,
> Since naught's so stockish, hard, and full of rage
> But music for the time doth change his nature.
> The man that hath no music in himself
> Nor is not moved with concord of sweet sounds,
> Is fit for treasons, stratagems, and spoils.
> The motions of his spirit are dull as night
> And his affections dark as Erebus.
> Let no such man be trusted. Mark the music.
>
> (5.1.70–88)

Innuendoes of *musica mundana*, golden, silent, and inaccessible, are intimated at Belmont, where actual music is heard, and where the Venetian incompatibilities of gold and love are finally reconciled, almost as much in the golden music as in the golden ring.

In *Twelfth Night*, however, the role of music is so obviously fundamental to the spirit of the play that it is momentarily surprising to find so little speculative music brought up for discussion. But I think that, on consideration of the nature of the play itself, the place of both active and intellectual music, and the relations between them, emerge as something far more complex than Shakespeare had hitherto cause to employ. *Twelfth Night* is, in very serious ways, a play about parties and what they do to people. Full of games, revels, tricks, and disguises, it is an Epiphany play, a ritualized Twelfth Night festivity in itself, but it is much more than this: the play gives us an analysis, as well as a representation, of feasting. It develops an ethic of indulgence based on the notion that the personality of any individual is a function not of the static proportions of the humors within him, but of the dynamic appetites that may more purposefully, as well as more pragmatically, be said to govern his behavior. Superficially close to comedy of humors in the characterological extremes of its dramatis personae, the play nevertheless seems almost intent on destroying the whole theory of comedy and of morality entailed by the comedy of humors.

The nature of revels is disclosed in the first scene. The materials are to be music, food and drink, and love. The basic action of both festivity in general, and of the play itself, is declared to be that of so surfeiting the appetite that it will sicken and die, leaving fulfilled the tempered, harmonious self. The movement of the whole play is that of a party: from appetite, through the direction of that appetite outward toward something, to satiation, and eventually to the condition when, as the Duke hopes for Olivia, "liver, brain and heart / These sovereign thrones, are all supplied, and filled / Her sweet perfections with one self king." The "one self king" is the final harmonious state to be achieved by each reveller, but it is also, in both the Duke's and Olivia's case, Cesario who kills "the flock of all affections else" that live in them, and who is shown forth in a literal Epiphany in the last act.

The Duke's opening speech describes both the action of feasting, and his own abundant, ursine, romantic temperament. But it also contains within it an emblematic representation of the action of surfeiting:

> If music be the food of love, play on.
> Give me excess of it, that, surfeiting,
> The appetite may sicken, and so die.
> That strain again! It had a dying fall.
> Oh, it came o'er my ear like the sweet sound
> That breathes upon a bank of violets,
> Stealing and giving odor! Enough, no more.
> 'Tis not so sweet now as it was before.
>
> (1.1.1–8)

The one personage in the play who remains a melancholic humors character is the one person who is outside the revels and cannot be affected by them. Olivia's rebuke cuts to the heart of his nature: "Thou art sick of self love, Malvolio, and taste with a distempered appetite." Suffering from a kind of moral indigestion, Malvolio's true character is revealed in his involuted, Puritanic sensibility that allows of no appetites directed outward. His rhetoric is full of the Devil; it is full of humors and elements as well. No other character tends to mention these save in jest, for it is only Malvolio who believes in them. Yet real, exterior fluids of all kinds, wine, tears, seawater, urine, and finally the rain of inevitability bathe the whole world of Illyria, in constant reference throughout the play.

The general concern of *Twelfth Night*, then, is *musica humana*, the Boethian application of abstract order and proportion to human behavior. The literalization of the universal harmony that is accomplished in comedy of humors, however, is unequivocally rejected. "Does not our life consist of the four elements?" catechizes Sir Toby. "Faith, so they say," replies Sir Andrew, "but I think it rather consists of eating and drinking." "Thou'rt a scholar," acknowledges Sir Toby. "Let us therefore eat and drink." "Who you are and what you would are out of my welkin—I might say 'element,' but the word is overworn," says Feste, who, taking offense at Malvolio's characterization of him as a "dry fool," touches off the whole proceedings against the unfortunate steward. The plot to ridicule Malvolio is more than the frolicsome revenge of an "allowed fool"; it serves both to put down the killjoy and to affirm the psychology of appetite and fulfillment that governs the play. To the degree that the *musica humana* of *Twelfth Night* involves the substitution of an alternative view to the fairly standard sixteenth-century descriptions of the order of the passions, an application of the musical metaphor would be trivial, and perhaps misleading. But the operation of practical music in the plot, the amazingly naturalistic treatment of its various forms, and the conclusions implied as to the nature and effects of music in both the context of celebration and in the world at large all result in some musical speculation that remains one of the play's unnoticed accomplishments.

The actual music in *Twelfth Night* starts and finishes the play, occurring throughout on different occasions and in different styles. The presumably instrumental piece in which the Duke wallows at the opening dampens his desire for it very quickly, but that desire returns before the play is over. Orsino's appetite at the start of the play is purportedly for Olivia, who hungers for, and indulges herself in, her own grief. The Duke's actual love, too, is for his own act of longing, and for his own exclamations of sentiment. The desires of both are directed outward before the play is over. But until a peculiar musical mechanism, which will be mentioned later on, has been set to work, the Duke will hunt his own heart; and his desires, "like fell and cruel hounds," will continue to pursue him. The music in act 2, scene 4, is of just such a nature to appease the Duke's extreme sentimentality. Orsino makes it plain what sort of song he wants to hear:

> Now, good Cesario, but that piece of song,
> That old and antique song we heard last night.
> Methought it did relieve my passion much,
> More than light airs and recollected terms
> Of these most brisk and giddy-paced times.
>
> (2.4.2–6)

This is a familiar sentimental attitude, the desire for the Good Old Song that nudges the memory, the modern request made of the cocktail pianist, the half-ironic translation in Bertolt Brecht's *Happy End*, where a singer tries to recapture better days by imploring "*Joe, mach die Musik von damals nach.*" Orsino's favorite song, he says,

>   is old and plain.
> The spinsters and the knitters in the sun
> And the free maids that weave their thread with bones
> Do use to chant it. It is silly, sooth,
> And dallies with the innocence of love,
> Like the old age.
>
> (2.4.44–49)

Actually, the song that Feste sings him is a highly extravagant, almost parodic version of the theme of death from unrequited love. Its rather stilted diction and uneasy prosody are no doubt intended to suggest a song from an old miscellany. "Come away" is a banal beginning, appearing at the start of four song texts in Canon Fellowes's collection. We may also presume that the setting employed was rather more archaic than that of the well-polished lute accompaniments of the turn of the century.

It is just one of these "light airs and recollected terms," however, with which Sir Toby and Feste plague Malvolio in their big scene of carousal (2.3). A setting of "Farewell, dear heart" appears in Robert Jones's first book of airs, published in 1600. Of the other songs in the same scene, one is a catch, a more trivial form of song, certainly with respect to its text, than the sophisticated and intricate lewdness of the post-Restoration round. The other is a "love song" sung by Feste, and preferred by Sir Toby and Sir Andrew to "a song of good life," perhaps with a pious text. It is of the finest type of Shakespearean song that catches up the spirit of overall themes and individual characters, ironically and prophetically pointing to the end of a plot or bit of action. All of "Oh mistress mine" is in one sense an invocation to Olivia to put off her self-indulgent grief, her courting of her dead brother's memory. In particular, the first stanza refers to Viola, the boy-girl true love, "that can sing both high and low."

Feste's songs to Malvolio in his madman's prison are both of an archaic cast. The first is a snatch of a song of Wyatt's, "A robyn, joly robyn" that was set to music by William Cornishe during the reign of Henry VIII. The other one, a parting jibe at Malvolio's cant about the Devil, suggests the doggerel of an old morality, invoking Malvolio as the Devil himself, and continuing the game of mocking him by appealing to his own rhetoric.

All of these occurrences of practical music function in the plot as well as with respect to the general theme of feasting and revels. The one reference to *musica speculativa* is a very interesting one, however, and leads to the most important aspect of the operation of music in *Twelfth Night*. Olivia is exhorting Viola to refrain from mentioning the Duke to her, and implying that she would rather be courted by his messenger:

> I bade you never speak of him again.
> But would you undertake another suit,
> I had rather hear you to solicit that
> Than music from the spheres.
>
> (3.1.118–21)

The citation of the music of the spheres here has the tone of most such references during the later seventeenth century in England. With the exception of poets like Milton and Marvell, who used metaphors from the old cosmology for intricate poetic purposes of their own, the music of the spheres became, in Cavalier and Augustan poetry, a formal compliment, empty of even the metaphorical import that the world view of the centuries preceding had given to it. Just as the word "heavenly," used in exclamations of praise, long ago became divorced from its substantive root, the music of the spheres gradually came to designate the acme of effective charm in a performer. It was often employed in compliments to ladies, for example, whose skill at singing made the spheres sound dissonant, abashed the singing angels, and so forth. As in the case of Dryden's music that would "untune the sky," references to the heavenly harmony had nothing to do with received ideas of music's importance during the later seventeenth century, which were more and more becoming confined to a rhetorical ability to elicit passion, on the one hand, and to provide ornament to the cognitive import of a text, on the other. Purcell likens music and poetry to beauty and wit, respectively; the former can unite to produce the same wondrous effects in song that the latter can in a human being, although the virtues of each are independent. The differences between music and poetry also tended to cluster about the celebrated rift between thought and feeling. Most important of all, traditional *musica speculativa* gradually ceased being a model of universal order, and was replaced by a notion of music as a model of rhetoric, whose importance lay in its ability to move the passions, rather than in its older role of the microcosmic copy of universal harmony. The Apollonian lute-harp-lyre constellation, once an emblem of reason and order, became an instrument of passion in the hands of Caravaggio's leering boys, and in the hands of Crashaw's musician who slew the nightingale by musically ravishing her, as even her avatar Philomela was never so ravished, to death.

With these considerations in mind, the crucial role to Viola as an instrument of such a rhetorical music becomes quite clear. It is unfortunate that we have no precise indication of an earlier version of the play, presumably rewritten when the superior singer Robert Armin entered Shakespeare's company, in which some of the songs may have been assigned to Viola. She declares herself at the outset:

> I'll serve this Duke.
> Thou shalt present me as a eunuch to him.
> It may be worth thy pains, for I can sing,
> And speak to him in many sorts of music,
> That will allow me very worth his service.
>
> (1.2.55–59)

She will be the Duke's instrument, although she turns out to be an instrument that turns in his hand, charming both Olivia and himself in unexpected fashion. Orsino is given an excess of music in Viola. As Cesario, she wins Olivia for her *alter ego* Sebastian; the latter is, himself, in his few scenes, rhetorically effective almost to the point of preciosity, and is likened to the musician Arion, who charmed his way to safety. Viola represents affective, instrumental, prematurely Baroque music in *Twelfth Night*, and it is she whose charm kills off the gourmandizing sentimentality in both Orsino and Olivia, directing their appetites of love outward, in fact, toward herself. Among the characters to whom Malvolio refers as "the lighter people," it is Feste, the singer and prankster, whose pipe and tabor serve as a travesty of Viola's vocal cords. The operation of Viola's "music" involves charming by the use of appearances; the effects of the trickery instigated by Feste are to make Malvolio appear, until he is undeceived, to be Olivia's ridiculously amorous swain. (It is, of course, the phrase "To be Count

Malvolio" that appears on his lips after reading the forged letter.) Through the mechanism of fooling, the travesty of music below stairs, Sir Andrew is chastened, Sir Toby is soberly married to Maria, Malvolio is made to act out the madness of which he falsely accused Feste, and "the whirligig of time brings in his revenges."

The music that brings about the conclusion of the revels is thus a figurative music. It pervades the symbolic enactment of indulgence and surfeit in the plot as the actual music, relegated to its several uses and forms with considerable eye to details of practice in Shakespeare's own day, pervades the spectacle of *Twelfth Night*. The play is about revelry, and, in itself, revels; so too, there is music in it, and a working out of a theme in speculative music that strangely coincides with later views on the subject. The *Ursprung* of Viola's music is certainly in the action of the play; it is not to be implied that *Twelfth Night* is anything of a formal treatise. The music in Illyria all serves its immediately dramatic purposes. Within the context of the play's anti-Puritan, anti-Jonsonian treatment of moral physiology, the role of music seems to have become inexorably defined for Shakespeare. Set in a framework of what, at this point, it might be almost coy to call a study in *musica humana*, practical music becomes justified in itself. Free of even the scraps of traditional musical ideology that had been put to use in the plays preceding it, *Twelfth Night* represents a high point in one phrase of Shakespeare's musical dramaturgy. It is not until *Antony and Cleopatra* and the last romances that the use of an almost supernatural music, perhaps, as has been suggested, imported to some degree from the musical *données* of the masque, comes to be associated with the late, great themes of reconciliation and transformation.

Malvolio and Class Ideology in *Twelfth Night*

Elliot Krieger

"The Morality of Indulgence"

In 1959 C. L. Barber's book *Shakespeare's Festive Comedy* and John Hollander's article "*Twelfth Night* and the Morality of Indulgence" challenged, with similar arguments, Morris P. Tilley's long-accepted thesis that *Twelfth Night* advocates a mean between extremes. Tilley saw *Twelfth Night* as "a philosophical defense of a moderate indulgence in pleasure, in opposition on the one hand to an extreme hostility to pleasure and on the other hand to an extreme self-indulgence." Hollander reacted against the entire tendency to place *Twelfth Night*, to find a moral "position" for the play. Hollander argued that in *Twelfth Night* Shakespeare substituted "what one might call a moral process for a moral system," that the "essential action" of this moral process is

> to so surfeit the Appetite upon excess that it "may sicken and so die." It is the Appetite, not the whole Self, however, which is surfeited: the Self will emerge at the conclusion of the action from where it has been hidden. The movement of the play is toward this emergence of humanity from behind a mask of comic type.

This "action," according to Hollander, ensures that Orsino, "embodying the overpowering appetite for romantic love," Olivia, "despite herself, a private glutton," and Sir Toby, with his "huge stomach for food and

---

From *A Marxist Study of Shakespeare's Comedies*. © 1979 by Elliot Krieger. Barnes & Noble, 1979.

drink" all "[kill] off" an "excessive appetite through indulgence of it" and supply the "liver, brain, and heart," with "one self king" (1.1.37–39). Each protagonist surfeits his or her "misdirected voracity" and thereby achieves "rebirth of the unencumbered self." Hollander argued that "everybody" achieves this rebirth: Orsino is supplied with Viola, "his fancy's queen," Olivia with "Cesario or king," "Toby and Maria are married, Aguecheek chastened, etc."

The supposed inclusiveness of Hollander's process—note how his "etc" hedges—depends on his assumption that Feste and Malvolio remain "outside the action" or are "left unaccounted for," that neither "has doffed his mask of feasting." Hollander asserted that Feste, who "represents" the "very nature" of the action is "unmotivated by any appetite, and is never sated of his fooling," and that Malvolio, who "alone is not possessed of a craving directed outward" is the only character who "cannot morally benefit from a period of self-indulgence."

Barber's argument was a little more abstract, and its thesis, that *Twelfth Night* "moves . . . through release to clarification," depended on the context that his book established. Yet Barber, like Hollander, presupposed that *Twelfth Night* does not demonstrate a static mean between extremes but enacts a movement toward excess that, reaching an extreme point, restores the social order of the play to its healthy norm. Barber's analysis of *Twelfth Night* derives from his assumption that

> just as a saturnalian reversal of social roles need not threaten the social structure, but can serve instead to consolidate it, so a temporary, playful reversal of sexual roles can renew the meaning of the normal relation. One can add that with sexual or with other relations, it is when the normal is secure that playful aberration is benign.

The "security" out of which the festive release emerges is essential to Barber's analysis of *Twelfth Night*. Barber argued that *Twelfth Night* exhibits "the use and abuse of social liberty"; but he qualified "liberty" by a subtle reference to social class: "the play exhibits the liberties which gentlemen take with decorum in the pursuit of pleasure and love."

The word *gentlemen* opens a whole realm of thought that Hollander excludes and that Barber overlooks. By loosely applying the moral process he has abstracted from the play to the play as a whole, instead of to selected characters within the play, Hollander managed to ignore completely the social distinctions that *Twelfth Night* so obviously delineates. He can argue that because Orsino and Olivia have external objects for their appetites, whereas Malvolio loves only himself, Malvolio's indulgence is "perverted" rather than "excessive," and consequently that Malvolio does not deserve "rebirth of the unencumbered self," "fulfillment" in "one self king": "His story effectively and ironically underlines the progress towards this fulfillment in everybody else, and helps to delineate the limitations of the moral domain of the whole play." Hollander gives little attention either to Viola's indulgence or to her fulfillment. He asserts, unconvincingly, that to indulge "she commits" herself to the love-game with Olivia "with redoubled force" and he assumes that to be "Orsino's mistress" will fulfill her "liver, brain, and heart." He supposes that Sebastian has "no real identity apart from Viola." Hollander has little or nothing to say regarding the fulfillment any of the other characters find at the conclusion. In fact, the particular moral process that Hollander has so eloquently described in the abstract does not, when applied to the characters and action of *Twelfth Night*, seem "to encompass everybody": Orsino, Olivia, and perhaps Sir Toby indulge, surfeit, and emerge; but Viola and Sebastian emerge without having indulged, Malvolio indulges and is, according to Hollander, justifiably submerged. The other characters are left out of the process and out of account.

When we apply the abstractions of Hollander's analysis to the characters within the play, we can see that the "morality of indulgence" applies to and protectively circumscribes the ruling class of *Twelfth Night*. According to Hollander, the excessive behavior that is moral when enacted by Orsino, Olivia, and Sir Toby is "perverted" when enacted by Malvolio. In fact, however, Malvolio's self-love differs from the obviously narcissistic preoccupations of Orsino and Olivia and the egoistic revelry of Sir Toby *only* because decorum forbids one of his rank to "surfeit on himself." Hollander correctly notes that the play does not praise Malvolio "as an example of righteous bourgeois opposition to medieval hierarchies," for Malvolio accepts degree—he opposes only his subordinate position within an hierarchical society. The play, however, does not dramatize strategies of bourgeois opposition so much as of aristocratic protection. Only a privileged social class has access to the morality of indulgence: if the members of the ruling class find their identities through excessive indulgence in appetite, the other characters in the play either work to make indulgence possible for their superiors or else, indulging themselves, sicken and so die.

Barber, like Hollander, deftly sidesteps the issue of social class in his discussion of festive release in *Twelfth Night*, although his descriptions of liberty and festivity seem continually to point toward acknowledgement of social privilege:

What enables Viola to bring off her role in disguise is her perfect
courtesy, . . . Her mastery of courtesy goes with her being the
daughter of "that Sebastian of Messalina whom I know you
have heard of": gentility shows through her disguise;

or:

Sir Toby is gentlemanly liberty incarnate, a specialist in it. . . .
Because Sir Toby has "faith"—the faith that goes with belonging—he does not need to worry when Maria teases him about
confining himself "within the modest limits of order."

Barber, however, does not pursue the social aspects of his observations, and
the principle of festive release remains, as throughout Barber's book, abstracted from the class relations that constitute its context. Because he ab-
stracts festivity from the class relations in the drama, Barber ignores the
effect that social class has on the definitions and applications of such key
terms as *courtesy* (in regard to Viola), *liberty* (in regard to Feste), and *decorum*
(in regard to Malvolio). For Feste, Barber writes, to "sing and beg"—that
is, to work and be dependent—constitutes a "liberty based on accepting
disillusion." Barber distinguishes Malvolio's desire "to violate decorum,"
to rise in stature, from true "liberty" because Malvolio wants to enjoy the
authority that accompanies stature, to "relish to the full" the "power"
decorum has "over others." The "liberty" of saturnalia, therefore, contrary
to Barber's premise, does not reverse social roles, in that the authority
relinquished by the ruling class cannot be enjoyed by the subservients because that violation of decorum would contrast with the "genuine, free
impulse" with which the ruling class asserts its authority. The violation of
decorum must, according to Barber, be treated "as a kind of foreign body
to be expelled by laughter."

We cannot really understand festive release or the morality of indulgence until we remove these categories from the realm of abstraction as
pure movement or process, place them within social categories, and see that
they emerge from the play so as to allow the aristocracy to achieve social
consolidation. In other words, we must redefine the moral process as a
ruling-class ideology. Each character in *Twelfth Night* embodies a particular
individual action—retreat, disguise, aspiration—taken within an hierarchic
society. These actions, separate strategies for achieving or asserting identity, when taken together dramatize the social conditions and consequences
that circumscribe each individual action. *Twelfth Night*, as a unified action,
distinguishes the strategies from one another, the luxury of aristocratic

retreat from the catastrophe of a servant's aspirations. Those who talk about movement, process, strategy, sympathy, or essential action outside of the social distinctions that the play maintains censor the ideological aspect of the play. In fact, the social distinctions do not form incidental aspects of a fairy tale romance; they are essential to the plot and theme of *Twelfth Night*.

"To Be Count Malvolio"

Surely, according to most readers of *Twelfth Night*, Malvolio represents the spirit of bourgeois independence. Although few would argue that through Malvolio Shakespeare satirically portrays a Puritan, most accept that Malvolio embodies the modern emphasis on economy, that, as Oscar James Campbell has written, Malvolio is "an enemy to the time-honored English hospitality and liberality because of the strain it puts upon his lady's purse." To an extent, Malvolio seems a representative "modern," partially because he resists the traditional hospitality of the English great house that supports such aristocratic ne'er-do-wells as Sir Toby and Sir Andrew, more so because, in direct contrast with Feste, Malvolio finds his vocation to be a humiliation and, he hopes, a temporary restriction. "Art any more than a steward?" (2.3.114), Sir Toby taunts him; and I suppose that Malvolio probably thinks to himself—"Yes; I am Malvolio." His sense that he is not bound to his vocation or to his degree, but that he has some form of personal autonomy that can be recognized and rewarded by society anticipates the modern separation of self from vocation.

But Malvolio expresses aspiration quite differently from Maria. Maria works so as to maintain the two second-world environments, the willed freedoms from time, established separately by Sir Toby and by Olivia. Maria's aspiration grows out of and depends upon the quality of the work that she performs; she rises in class as a reward for her service. Malvolio's aspiration—"To be Count Malvolio!" (2.5.35)—does not depend on the work that he performs; he thinks of aspiration as a sudden elevation, a jump in class status that will occur because of the intervention of fortune (23) or of "Jove and my stars," (172). Malvolio, that is, has the fantasy that he will jump class not as a result of the actions within the everyday world of time that he is ordered to perform but through the transformation of the everyday world into a world of wish-fulfillment, of projected desire. The yellow stockings that he is asked to wear will not, he feels, win Olivia; they will merely seal the contract that Fortune has drawn up. His sense of aspiration, and concomitantly of his own self-worth, is a second-world fantasy, an attempt to transform the world of time and space into a leisured world structured around a personal whim, to replace environment with ego. In this regard, Malvolio absolutely opposes the ideal service embodied by Viola and Antonio: the ideal servant is vulnerable because treated like an object by the master; the aspiring servant—what might be called the subjective or the self-conscious servant—is vulnerable because he adopts aristocratic methods, the aristocratic attitude toward the material world, without the implicit protection from the hardships of the world guaranteed by aristocratic status.

Ultimately, there is no fundamental difference between Malvolio's fantasy of narcissistic withdrawal into a world in which he can be Count Malvolio, sitting in state, "having come from a day-bed" (45, 48) and Orsino's narcissistic withdrawal into the Petrarchan conventions and the beds of flowers. The two second-world fantasies differ only in the social reaction and response that they elicit. Those near Orsino confirm his withdrawal from time: they echo his language and thereby subordinate the world and their autonomy in the world to the Duke's ego, they assure Orsino that he is neither solitary nor mad. The social reaction to Malvolio's second world is just the opposite: others cut Malvolio off from the world, imprison him in darkness; they disconfirm his sense perceptions and accuse him of being mad. Certainly, madness pervades the play, but whereas Sir Toby and Orsino use madness as an indulgence, and Sebastian and Olivia find their wishes fulfilled in their madness, only Malvolio confronts madness as a restriction and a limitation.

Malvolio's imprisonment marks the limit that class status imposes on the "morality of indulgence." The fantasy that leads to Malvolio's imprisonment—his love for Olivia and his vision of himself as a Count—is not in the abstract ridiculous or perverse. Only when we apply the ruling-class assumptions about degree and decorum does it seem that Malvolio is sick of self-love, whereas Orsino and Olivia seem to engage in healthy, therapeutic folly and deceit. Nothing in the play supports Hollander's statement that Malvolio "alone is not possessed of a craving directed outward, towards some object on which it can surfeit and die; he alone cannot morally benefit from a period of self-indulgence." Such a statement merely represents the critic's wholehearted adoption of the aristocratic attitude toward an indulgence manifested by someone of inferior stature. Orsino, Olivia, and Sir Toby behave just as egocentrically as does Malvolio, and Malvolio, like them, directs his indulgence outward in order to gratify his ego and to expand his ego-centered world. But, Hollander argues, aristocratic indulgence is moral or, as others have said, an "education in matters of love," whereas Malvolio's indulgence is perverse (Hollander), a parody

(Jenkins), an extreme (Phialas), a violation of decorum and of the social order (Barber).

A ruling-class ideology operates within the play and prevents Malvolio from creating his own antithetic second world. The second world that Malvolio tries to create, however, is not antithetic to that ideology, for Malvolio accepts and supports the aristocratic assumptions about the need for respect, decorum, and propriety. The charge against Sir Toby—"Is there no respect of place, persons, nor time in you?" (2.3.91–92)—is retained, emphatically, in Malvolio's fantasy: "telling them I know my place as I would they should do theirs" (2.5.53–54). It is quite wrong to see Malvolio's fantasy as egalitarian or as a bourgeois opposition to aristocratic norms. Malvolio attends scrupulously to each aspect of aristocratic behavior, and in fact part of what he would hope to accomplish as Count Malvolio would be the "amendment" of Sir Toby's behavior, the restoration of Olivia's family to normality and decorum. Barber wrongly says that Malvolio has a "secret wish . . . to violate decorum himself." Rather, hoping to achieve the stature into which he was not born, Malvolio (perhaps, surprisingly, like Othello) profoundly respects the superficial accoutrements of rank, the display of decorum. Before he discovers Maria's forged letter Malvolio violates decorum only in that, while still a steward, he indulges aloud in his fantasies of aspiration. The enactment of fantasy must remain the aristocratic prerogative.

There is nothing tragic about Malvolio. The way his aspiration develops and is placed within the drama makes him, in fact, comic in the most elementary—the Bergsonian—sense of the word: he is a complex, dignified man who suddenly is reduced to a mechanism, an object. This reduction occurs when and because his private, second-world fantasy is drawn from him, brought from the world of ideas and mental abstractions out into the material world of time, actions, and community. The letter that Malvolio stoops to pick up marks, from his point of view, the boundary between these two worlds; his private (if overheard) fantasies take on objective status in the forged letter. The letter seems to Malvolio a license for an exclusively aristocratic privilege: to transform a private, narcissistic fantasy into public behavior. His narcissism does become public, enacted in the world, but the letter actually binds rather than licenses him: the letter prescribes Malvolio's actions to a set of imposed restrictions, rather than permits his behavior to be, in true second-world fashion, modulated only by his changeable, subjective humour. The restrictions—the cross-garters, the enforced smiling, which so obviously go *against* his humour ("Sad, lady? I could be sad. This does make some obstruction in the blood, this cross-gartering, but what of that?" [3.4.20–22])—make him comic, largely because at the very moment at which he feels that he is at last enacting his subjective fantasies, we are aware that, more than ever, he is being manipulated, treated like an object.

When being treated like an object, Malvolio is in effect restored to his place within the social hierarchy. Malvolio's reduction moves in the exact opposite way from Viola's restoration of stature and thereby of autonomy. Viola helps to maintain and to confirm the whims and fantasies of her master, and she does so in part as a mediated expression of her love for him. Malvolio enacts his own fantasies, as an *immediate* expression of his love for Olivia. Temporarily, Viola's willed subordination and Malvolio's willed aspiration have the same effect: both Viola and Malvolio become objectified, imprisoned within the role of servant. When her aristocratic identity is discovered or revealed, however, Viola's objectification reverses, and Orsino acknowledges her as an equal, her "master's mistress" (5.1.326); Viola becomes a subjective participant in the social ceremonies of and beyond the conclusion. Malvolio, however, has his sanity discovered or revealed only to be confirmed as an object of laughter—"the most notorious geck and gull / That e'er invention play'd on" (343–44)—and, for Feste, of revenge (376–77). The conclusion of *Twelfth Night* contains an element of the Patient Griselda myth—complete subservience leads to unexpected elevation—as qualified by the aristocratic face behind Viola's subordinate mask; essentially, however, the conclusion confirms the aristocratic fantasy (Maria is, discreetly, kept off-stage) that clarification is achieved when people are released from indulgence and restored to the degree of greatness with which they were born.

Nature's Bias

Ruth Nevo

Twelfth Night has been called a "masterpiece of recapitulation." Twins, reunions, rivalries, love's tamings and matings, mistakings and unmaskings, the ladder of language upon whose lower rungs ambitious nitwits bark their skinny shins, a (finally) domesticated Falstaffian rogue, an impostor whose posturing is an oblique and distorted mirror image of the protagonists' besetting deficiencies (even his name is a dark anagram of his mistress's), the page disguise, the partnership of lady and mocking fool. It is familiar Shakespeare country, and the Terentian itinerary is familiar, too, save in one important respect. There are no interfering or match-making parents in *Twelfth Night*, as there are virtually none in *As You Like It* as well. Rosalind's father, important as he is . . . is not to be thought of while there are young men like Orlando about in the forest, and the father of the Illyrian twins provides no more than the canonical mode for identifications. Fathers will return, to be sure, in the tragedies and the romances, but they are at present in eclipse, leaving the field to the initiatives and the entanglements of their daughters, and when these are scarcely adequate, to great creating Nature herself. As Sebastian says:

> So come it, lady, you have been mistook;
> But Nature to her bias drew in that
>
> (5.1.259–60)

and truly a creative and providential musicianship is required to compose the oceanic Illyrian eros, as Illyria's Duke intimates in his very first speech:

From *Comic Transformation in Shakespeare*. © 1980 by Ruth Nevo. Methuen, 1980.

> If music be the food of love, play on,
> Give me excess of it; that surfeiting,
> The appetite may sicken, and so die.
> That strain again, it had a dying fall;
> O, it came o'er my ear like the sweet sound
> That breathes upon a bank of violets,
> Stealing and giving odor. Enough, no more,
> 'Tis not so sweet now as it was before.
> O spirit of love, how quick and fresh art thou,
> That notwithstanding thy capacity
> Receiveth as the sea, nought enters there,
> Of what validity and pitch soe'er,
> But falls into abatement and low price
> Even in a minute.
>
> (1.1.1–14)

Illyria, it will be remembered, is sea-girt. Not only are the twins cast up out of the ocean, and the impression of a coastal town maintained in the idiom of the inhabitants: "Will you hoist sail, sir?" says Maria, for instance, to the snubbed Viola (1.5.202); we also have two sea captains in assiduous attendance, and imagery of the "hungry sea" presenting itself constantly to the protagonists' imaginations.

The first exchange between Orsino and his entourage advances considerably our understanding of what is deficient, imperfect or wanting in Illyria. Orsino is restless, dissatisfied, vacillating between moods, introspective to a degree, with a mind full of shapes, but without an object upon which his mind can rest and with which his desire can engage. And Curio, whose name is significant, as is Valentine's—we note that the names of these two servitors of Orsino's suggest connoisseurship in what the Victorians called the tender passion—provides our next clue.

> CURIO. Will you go hunt, my lord?
> DUKE. What, Curio?
> CURIO. The hart.
> DUKE. Why, so I do, the noblest that I have.
>   O, when mine eyes did see Olivia first,
>   Methought she purg'd the air of pestilence!
>   That instant was I turn'd into a hart,
>   And my desires, like fell and cruel hounds,
>   E'er since pursue me.
>
> (1.1.16–23)

The Duke's reply informs us of Olivia. But it also informs us of Orsino's self-image. Before the hunting metaphor is over, it is Orsino who is transformed into a pursued creature, not Olivia. He is Actaeon, turned into a stag and pursued by the hounds of his desire. "How will she love," sighs Orsino, "when the rich golden shaft / Hath kill'd the flock of all affections else / That live in her;" (1.1.34). This is an image which neatly joins the double face of venery, phallic and predatory. But it is to sweet beds of flowers that the Duke returns, to be alone in the delicious auto-eroticism of love thoughts and the high fantastical images they generate.

It is common in the criticism to hear of the malaise of Illyria as having to do with sentimentality, affectation, infatuation, narcissism. It is, says Jon S. Lawry, "a land transfixed in self love." "Orsino glories in the proper fickleness and moodiness" of the love-sick swain, and is [according to Joseph H. Summers] "unaware that he is in love with love rather than with a person." Olivia is in similar case, and only in Viola and Sebastian do we find "a love as honest and spring-like as Illyria's is affected and wintry" [Lawry]. Jan Kott on the other hand, takes an antithetical view which stresses the symbolic import of the sex-disguise. "The real theme of Illyria," as of the Sonnets, he says, "is erotic delirium, or the metamorphoses of sex . . . the impossibility of choice between the youth and the woman, the fragile boundary between friendship and love . . . the universality of desire which cannot be contained in or limited to one sex."

I wish to argue for a *via media* between these two views grounded in the discovery of Shakespeare's unfolding comic form which analysis of his early comedies allows us to make. The formula which comes closest to the theory of Shakespeare's deep structure which I have been pressing in these pages is Barber's "through release to clarification," but oddly enough his own chapter on *Twelfth Night*—"Testing Courtesy and Humanity" does not seem to me to grapple with the central issues of the play. A closer examination of the comic process of imbalance and excess, of preposterous fantasy, of disinhibition and of re-equilibrium is required.

Before the first act is over we shall have been given striking insights into the comic disposition in Illyria, which subsequent events will bear out.

"How will she love," sighs Orsino, "when the rich golden shaft / Hath kill'd the flock of all affections else / That live in her" (1.1.34). As has been noted, it is a truculent, masculine, predatory image. But when he sends his proxy page to pay court on his behalf, it is, strangely, on account of the page's youthful nubility, his harmless tenderness of aspect. One might well have expected an amatory ambassador to be more self-assertive than his client, not less. But Cesario will be a suitable suppliant, Orsino feels:

For they shall yet belie thy happy years,
That say thou art a man. Diana's lip
Is not more smooth and rubious; thy small pipe
Is as the maiden's organ, shrill and sound,
And all is semblative a woman's part.

(1.4.30–34)

The speech tells us much: of the way Orsino conceives of the role of suitor; of what he imagines the wishes of the lady he is wooing to be; and of those features of his new page which have caught his eye and noticeably advanced the page in his affections.

It is the femininity of his young page which appeals to him, but not, I submit, in narcissistic attraction to a quality his own nature shares. As has already been observed, Orsino is Shakespeare's latest embodiment of the courtly-love convention. He is conducting his amorous affairs in the style of woeful and love-lorn Petrarchanism which had been the target of the satirical mockery of Speed, Moth and Ganymede himself. He is Silvius in *As You Like It* writ large. He is, it will be noticed, conservative in his tastes, nostalgic for the old age, and scornful of these "most brisk and giddy-paced times" (2.4.6). He is, in a way, a Don Quixote as out of joint with his times as that good Knight was with the very same times. Or, as was the doting and chivalric Don Armado, who did not enjoy any noticeable success with Jacquenetta. In the realistically conceived Elizabethan milieu of *Twelfth Night* the suppliant posture is easily made to appear ineffectual and even effeminate. In *As You Like It*, too, it will be remembered, the meek entreaties of Silvius did not fare well with the high-handed Phebe, who, for her part, promptly fell in love with the swashbuckling airs and demonstratively non-feminine demeanour of Ganymede. Shakespeare, it seems, is using the outworn Petrarchan postures that Orsino strikes to characterize the deficiency in him, at any rate vis-à-vis Olivia, of a sufficiently masculine self-assertiveness.

The portrait of Orsino is subtly drawn; as subtly as is that of Olivia. They are both in unstable tension with themselves, Olivia through the exigencies of her circumstances, Orsino through a degree of self-delusion or misguidedness regarding his own nature and his role as lover.

Fatherless and brotherless, Olivia is the sole mistress of her household. She is its source of authority, and her unruly house guests are there to show that she is able to take command, though the turbulence below stairs under Sir Toby's aegis indicates that her control is not impregnable. She leans upon her steward in her lonely eminence, and not only to ward off a suit from the count (1.5.109). But her even-handed distribution of remonstrance and consolation to the former shows her not inconsiderable capacity for mastery:

> OLIVIA. O, you are sick of self-love Malvolio, and taste with a
> distemper'd appetite. To be generous, guiltless, and of
> free disposition, is to take those things for bird-bolts that
> you deem cannon-bullets. There is no slander in an
> allowed fool, though he do nothing but rail; nor no
> railing in a known discreet man, though he do nothing
> but reprove.
>
> (1.5.90–96)

Interestingly enough, Sebastian later argues for her sanity in an apparently mad world on the grounds that otherwise

> She could not sway her house, command her followers,
> Take and give back affairs, and their dispatch,
> With such a smooth, discreet, and stable bearing
> As I perceive she does.
>
> (4.3.17–20)

But that this is not the sole dedication of her life is perhaps indicated by the shrewd Feste's ironically appreciative acknowledgement of her defence of fools, in the form of an offhand blessing upon his madonna's future maternity: "Thou has spoke for us, madonna, as if thy eldest son should be a fool; whose skull Jove cram with brains! for—here he comes—one of thy kin has a most weak *pia mater*" (1.5.112–15).

Moreover, "She'll none o' th' Count," Toby tells Andrew. "She'll not match above her degree, neither in estate, years, nor wit; I have heard her swear't. Tut, there's life in't, man" (1.3.109–11). No word here of the mourning. True, the rich jest here lies in Toby's poker-faced encouragement of Andrew's hopes for a match with his wealthy niece, a matter in which Toby has no small stake. But throughout the early scenes our impression grows that the cloistering of Olivia is just possibly a mourning of convenience to ward off an unwelcome suitor. And is it any wonder indeed, that this lady, gallantly and graciously and not without difficulty performing a man's role in her household, cannot fall in love with a Duke in whom the balance of the masculine and feminine is diametrically discordant to her own? She supposes him virtuous, knows him noble, of great estate, of fresh and stainless youth, good reputation, free, learned, valiant and handsome (2.1.258–62). Yet she cannot love him.

Viola's arrival upon the coast of Illyria reveals, however, a degree of ambivalence in her behaviour as well as in Olivia's. "O that I served that lady," she exclaims when she hears of the latter's loss of father and brother. But she does not fly to the Countess Olivia for succour, woman to woman, despite her sympathy for a fellow-mourner. Instead she chooses to be adventurously epicene in the Duke's entourage. Viola escapes her feminine state but at the cost of a (symbolic) castration: it is as a eunuch (to account for her voice) that she will "sing / And speak to him in many sorts of music" (1.2.57); Olivia, cloistered for a dead brother's love, suffers a real incarceration.

The play thus invites us to perceive a degree of instability or volatility in the perception of themselves of all these three protagonists. This being so, no play of Shakespeare's is launched with greater dispatch into its vortex of truth-discovering deceptions than this. Act 1, scene 4, already finds the disguised Viola a reluctant ambassador, on behalf of her deceived employer:

> I'll do my best
> To woo your lady. [*Aside*] Yet a barful strife!
> Whoe'er I woo, myself would be his wife.
>   (1.4.40–42)

The great embassy scene in act 1 is prepared for by Malvolio's acidulous reply to Olivia's question concerning the stubborn messenger:

> OLIVIA. Of what personage and years is he?
> MALVOLIO. Not yet old enough for a man, nor young enough
>   for a boy; as a squash is before 'tis a peascod, or a
>   codling when 'tis almost an apple. 'Tis with him in
>   standing water, between boy and man. He is very well-
>   favor'd, and he speaks very shrewishly. One would think
>   his mother's milk were scarce out of him.
>   (1.5.155–62)

And presently we observe that he speaks very shrewishly indeed, and with a blend of urbane irony, provocative impertinence and taut vulnerability which might well catch attention harder to catch than that of the Lady Olivia. Both ladies are veiled in the encounter and the drama therefore takes place in the audience's mind on two distinct levels. What we watch is a wit combat in which each side gives as good as she gets. The text of Orsino's bosom provides a prolegomenon, the unveiled picture of Olivia's face the centrepiece. "Excellently done, if God did all," says Viola (1.5.236), the impudence a mask, we infer, for a pang at the heart. Olivia's coolly unperturbed reply, " 'Tis in grain, sir, 'twill endure wind and weather" (1.5.237) produces the genuine, and generous, compliment of

> 'Tis beauty truly blent, whose red and white
> Nature's own sweet and cunning hand laid on.
> Lady, you are the cruell'st she alive
> If you will lead these graces to the grave,
> And leave the world no copy.
>
> (1.5.239–44)

Nothing could be less like the courtly hyperboles of Orsino's complaints to his disdainful beauty. This unaffected candour transcends finesses of courtship diplomacy. We know why: this really is woman to woman. But to Olivia's ears, we may suppose, the words of the new ambassador must possess a ring of undissimulated, disinterested, unconventionalized frankness totally new to her. The Lady Olivia retains her own urbane self-possession, however:

> O, sir, I will not be so hard-hearted; I will give out divers schedules of my beauty. It shall be inventoried, and every particle and utensil labell'd to my will: as, *item*, two lips, indifferent red; *item* two grey eyes, with lids to them: *item*, one neck, one chin, and so forth. Were you sent hither to praise me?
>
> (1.5.244–49)

until a reminder of Orsino's Petrarchan ardours—"adorations, fertile tears . . . groans that thunder love . . . sighs of fire" (1.5.255–56) causes her to reveal for a moment a chink in her armour. Her description of Orsino (1.5.258–63) (honey, no doubt, in the ears of his ambassador) is accompanied by the puzzlement, even the distress of "I cannot love him . . . But yet, I cannot love him." What does he lack, that, strangely enough, his cheeky ambassador apparently possesses, since the sisterly mourning ritual is cast aside in a trice after their first encounter?

It is her adventurous, plucky, give-as-good-as-you-get braggartry, we are invited to infer, that not only gains her entrance to the Lady Olivia, but captures the lady's heart. The touch of reckless forthrightness, the spirit, the candour, the imaginative panache with which the willow cabin fantasy is described and courtly compliment revivified in the loyal cantons of condemned love in which Cesario would "Hallow your name to the reverberate hills, / And make the babbling gossip of the air / Cry out 'Olivia'"! (1.5.272–74)—these are surely precisely the self-assertive, masculine qualities which have been lacking in Orsino and which promptly bring out the womanly Olivia, a "bringing out" in which discretion becomes impetuosity and composure disintegrates in distracted doting upon the Duke's peevish messenger.

But if the embassy thus brings about a speedy Nemesis upon Viola's hermaphrodite adventure, it also provides a rich source of information concerning her master's fluctuating self-image and with beautifully designed symmetry the undisguisable femininity of Cesario/Viola brings out in Orsino a new, mature and manly good sense.

It is a scene of intimate man-to-man confidences, during which Orsino advises his young companion regarding the desirable age of a wife. The latter's choice, "About your years, my Lord," would be

> Too old, by heaven. Let still the woman take
> An elder than herself, so wears she to him;
> So sways she level in her husband's heart.
> For, boy, however we do praise ourselves,
> Our fancies are more giddy and unfirm,
> More longing, wavering, sooner lost and worn,
> Than women's are.
>
> (2.4.29–35)

But it is a moment only. Orsino is in unstable equilibrium in his views of women, and sways from the normal male sex-object chauvinism of

> For women are as roses, whose fair flow'r
> Being once display'd doth fall that very hour
>
> (2.4.38–39)

to an inflated and self-regarding tirade in which he casts himself in the role of Neoplatonic courtier saint, and sweeps aside the claim made by Cesario for the integrity of the lady's affections in the case:

> There is no woman's sides
> Can bide the beating of so strong a passion
> As love doth give my heart; no woman's heart
> So big, to hold so much; they lack retention.
> Alas, their love may be call'd appetite,
> No motion of the liver, but the palate,
> That suffer surfeit, cloyment, and revolt,
> But mine is all as hungry as the sea,
> And can digest as much.
>
> (2.4.93–101)

The Duke's mind, as Feste says, is a very opal-changeable taffeta. But the changes can be charted. The encounters between the Duke and his page offer rich material for inference. When Orsino responds to Cesario's tale of a sister who pined for love with a green and yellow melancholy, smiling at grief, with the question: "But died thy sister of her love my boy?" it is not in mere curiosity or sudden sympathetic interest in the tale that I believe he speaks. It is a pressing, triumphant rhetorical question, which still harps upon the superiority of men as martyrs to love. The song he requested, it will be remembered, and which spurred him to renewed beseechings to his sovereign cruelty, was the complaint of a sad true lover, slain by a fair cruel maid.

We begin to understand Orsino's self-delusion. Olivia represents to him the sonneteer's lady he believes himself in love with, while what his nature truly needs and responds to is the youthful, dependent, and devoted femininity of Viola which is scarcely veiled by the page disguise. What we are thus invited to perceive in each of these protagonists is not merely illusion, posture or attitudinizing. They are each in a state of disequilibrium regarding masculine and feminine roles and impulses which they themselves misassess. And it is precisely the comic device, the misapprehensions it entails, the *processus turbarum* of tumult and preposterous complication which serves to bring out, and even exacerbate their latent sexual identities. In no play of Shakespeare's is the effect of the comic device, source of error and truth, more aptly therapeutic. It plunges them into misprision, fools them to the top of their bent, ties a "knot too hard for [Viola] to untie" but in the volatile process they are all released from the various traps—emotional or circumstantial—which prevent the benign fulfilment of their natures. For it is not that there is no consonance between temperament and self-image. Orsino is a touch effeminate, Olivia is masterful, Viola is headstrong. We have only to imagine characters dominated by these traits, growing fixed and embedded and compulsive in them, to be aware of the proximity of Jonsonian humours (in literature) or personality problems (in life) to this Illyrian fantasia.

But we do not need Jonson. We have Malvolio. Not to mention the feckless Andrew, who, though he has the back trick simply as strong as any man in Illyria, and was adored once, is perhaps as marvellously impenetrable to self-knowledge as any character in drama. The lower plot counterpoints the upper as in *A Midsummer Night's Dream* and *Love's Labour's Lost*, and its scenes are cunningly interspersed with those above stairs. Its practices are devised by the lively Maria, as witty a piece of Eve's flesh as any in

Illyria, as the disguise stratagem was devised by Viola, and both in subtle ways, unmask.

When we first observe Malvolio alone, unaware that he is being watched, he is practising behaviour to his shadow, and fantasizing, in a way that brings Sir Toby near to apoplexy, a marriage with Olivia:

> MALVOLIO. Having been three months married to her, sitting
>   in my state—
> SIR TOBY. O, for a stone-bow, to hit him in the eye!
> MALVOLIO. Calling my officers about me, in my branch'd
>   velvet gown; having come from a day-bed, where I had
>   left Olivia sleeping—
> SIR TOBY. Fire and brimstone!
> FABIAN. O, peace, peace!
> MALVOLIO. And then to have the humor of state; and after a
>   demure travel of regard—telling them I know my place
>   as I would they should do theirs—to ask for my kinsman
>   Toby—
> SIR TOBY. Bolts and shackles!
> FABIAN. O peace, peace, peace! Now, now.
> MALVOLIO. Seven of my people, with an obedient start, make
>   out for him. I frown the while, and perchance wind up
>   my watch, or play with my—some rich jewel. Toby
>   approaches; curtsies there to me—
> SIR TOBY. Shall this fellow live?
>
> (2.5.44–62)

That place and power are his obsessive motivations is plain to be seen, and neatly dramatized by the fingering of his steward's badge of office, which fantasy transforms to "some rich jewel." If the main protagonists are confused or in unstable equilibrium about their sexual identities, Malvolio can hardly be said to possess a *sexual* identity at all. It is surely not by chance that Maria's maxim, "Some are born great, some achieve greatness, and some have greatness thrust upon them" parodies the Gospel according to Matthew on the subject of marriage: "For there are some eunuchs, which were so born from their mother's womb; and there are some eunuchs, which were made eunuchs of men: and there be eunuchs, which have made themselves eunuchs for the kingdom of heaven's sake" (Matt. 19: 12). And Malvolio strutting and preening and being unctuously coy in yellow stockings and cross garters is doubly ludicrous to the extent that he is doubly deluded.

> OLIVIA. Why, how dost thou, man? What is the matter with
> thee?
> MALVOLIO. Not black in my mind, though yellow in my legs.
> It did come to his hands, and commands shall be
> executed. I think we do know the sweet Roman hand.
> OLIVIA. Wilt thou go to bed, Malvolio?
> MALVOLIO. To bed? Ay, sweet heart, and I'll come to thee.
> OLIVIA. God comfort thee! Why dost thou smile so, and kiss
> thy hand so oft?
>
> (3.4.24–33)

This caricature of a self-image totally unconsonant with the facts is repeated in the idiotic Aguecheek, who, though occasionally capable of regretting his over-expenditure of time in fencing, dancing and bear-baiting rather than in the arts, is never less than complacent about his achievements. His Nemesis will be the duel; Malvolio's the exorcism rites of Sir Topas, in which Feste's elegantly learned fooling and his pantomimic virtuosity magically create the madness imputed to the imprisoned steward:

> MALVOLIO. I am not mad, Sir Topas, I say to you this house is
> dark.
> CLOWN. Madman, thou errest. I say there is no darkness but
> ignorance, in which thou art more puzzled than the
> Egyptians in their fog.
> MALVOLIO. I say this house is as dark as ignorance, though
> ignorance were as dark as hell; and I say there was never
> man thus abus'd.
>
> (4.2.40–47)

It is customary in Shakespeare's comic tumults for things to get worse before they can get better. Impulses released must spin out of control, become preposterous or excessive before the system can reject or properly harmonize them. Thus Olivia hurls discretion to the winds in her pursuit of Cesario and in her precipitous marriage, which, added to Cesario's smooth and rubious lip brings out an excess of masculine aggressiveness in Orsino. The speech in act 5, scene 1, in which this is expressed is as packed and as menacing as anything in the tragedies still to be written:

> But this your minion, whom I know you love,
> And whom, by heaven I swear, I tender dearly,
> Him will I tear out of that cruel eye,
> Where he sits crowned in his master's spite.

Come boy, with me, my thoughts are ripe in mischief.
I'll sacrifice the lamb that I do love,
To spite a raven's heart within a dove.

(5.1.125–31)

It is a dangerous moment. It is the moment of incipient disaster, of incipient tragic possibility, for which the remedies in comic plots provide a providential salvation.

The remedy in *Twelfth Night* is, of course, the appearance of Sebastian, which closes the gap opened at the beginning of the play by his loss at sea—so far as Viola knew; and it is at the point in the narrative sequence when the comic device—Viola's disguise as a boy—is pretty well exhausted, unable to be useful any longer, that he reappears. The exhaustion of the device has been hilariously brought out by her *cri de coeur* when she is faced with the now unavoidable duel—"A little thing would make me tell them how much I lack of a man." She is saved by Antonio at that point so that Sebastian will be able to make his own appearance at precisely the moment in the sequence when it will be most effective, conclusive and clarifying.

It is an *anagnorisis* in the fullest sense. A recognition scene in which the characters' recognitions and the audiences' larger cognitions fall harmoniously into place. When Sebastian appears in act 5, scene 1, he supplies at once the brother Viola believes lost, the husband Olivia believes she has married, and the key to the mystery of the "dissembling cub" Orsino believes he has cherished to his own disadvantage. But what we have particularly to take in, and what precipitates our understanding of the play is more than this neat solution to the errors and mistaken identities caused by Viola's disguise. What I believe we are invited to take in is the unequivocal manliness of the young man Sebastian. He, as it appears from the broken coxcombs, has made his appearance as the "firago" both the dauntless duelsters believed the other to be. He has laid about him to such good effect that poor Andrew calls him the "very devil incardinate." True, Andrew's is perhaps not the last word on martial valour, but his broken pate and Toby's are there in evidence. Barber has noted that "To see this manly reflex is delightful—almost a relief. The particular implausibility that there should be an identical man to take Viola's place with Olivia is submerged in the general, beneficent realization that there is such a thing as a man." I would like to press the point further. Sebastian is the male figure that the play, one of Shakespeare's subtlest dramatizations of the battle of the sexes, needs: He embodies a proper masculinity and the proper playing of a masculine role.

It will be remembered that when we first see him in the company of

Antonio we witness his firm but gentle rejection of Antonio's passionate devotion—yet another mirror image of misdirected love:

> ANTONIO. If you will not murther me for my love, let me be your servant.
>
> SEBASTIAN. If you will not undo what you have done, that is, kill him whom you have recover'd, desire it not. Fare ye well at once; my bosom is full of kindness, and I am yet so near the manners of my mother, that upon the least occasion more mine eyes will tell tales of me.
>
> (2.1.35–42)

That he possesses sensibility, is no mere macho, the gentleness of these "manners of my mother" attests. And in this he is the perfect counterpart or double to his sister Viola in whose nature, too, the presence of a blend of feminine and masculine traits is potentially harmonious and benign.

Sexual identity has been in some way disordered, frustrated, displaced, diverted or deficient in every one of the chief dramatis personae, and in the chief buffoon-imposter Malvolio. It is this subtle imbalance of the personality as much as outward circumstances which has caused their "madness." It is this that the comic device entangles in absurdity, that is self-exposed and mocked in the counterpoint Malvolio plot, and that is caricatured in the sexless ninny Andrew. And it is the remedy to this manifold deficiency that is heralded and embodied by Sebastian. The entry of Sebastian is a living image of the sanguine masculinity that Viola, as cheeky Cesario, put on; that Olivia, a Penelope badgered by suitors, needed; that Andrew Aguecheek aped; that Malvolio pretended to, would have exploited and abused, and grotesquely fails to understand; and that Orsino, out-of-date lover, lacked, until his page brought it out in him.

Alexander Leggatt makes the excellent point that "in other comedies a single personality is extended by disguise, but the extension is temporary and finally withdrawn; this is the only case in which the new figure created by disguise has also an objective reality, a life of its own." This is in keeping, he maintains, with the miraculous birth the feast of the Epiphany celebrates, but I cannot agree with him when he says "the ending takes little account of the reasons for particular attachments; it is a generalised image of love." Neither this "generalization" nor Kott's Dionysian saturnalia celebrating "man's eternal dream of overcoming the boundaries of his own body and of his sex" seems to me to catch the brilliant individuality of *Twelfth Night*'s realization of the comic principle.

Feste's ministrations to Malvolio in prison travesty cure, though they have their own rough curative effect just as had Dr Pinch's in *The Comedy of Errors*. But the cure of souls that is conducted homeopathically at the main plot level is the peak achievement in the orchestration of comedy game and human comedy which crowns the early plays. When Orsino says to Viola

> Your master quits you; and for your service done him,
> So much against the mettle of your sex,
> So far beneath your soft and tender breeding,
> And since you called me master for so long,
> Here is my hand—you shall from this time be
> Your master's mistress
>
> (5.1.321–26)

the words reverberate retrospectively through the entire play, setting to rights Shakespeare's most finely conceived comic perversity, and resolving his most brilliant essay in comic remedies. Nor should the autumnal mood of Feste's final song disturb our pleasure in the play. Feste is the most detached, observant (his livelihood depends upon it) and ironic of Shakespeare's fools, and the tutelary spirit of a play whose marvellous fooling is as serious as it is funny. If he knows that no festivity can put a stop to time, this is not to detract from time's benign moments, but to make them doubly valuable.

Choosing the Right Mate in *Twelfth Night*

Coppélia Kahn

In [*The Comedy of*] *Errors*, the twin provides an affective bridge from filial to individual identity: seeking the twin, the hero finds his mate, but only when he is able to distinguish himself firmly from his twin. In *Twelfth Night*, we move a step further from the family, and the twin and other doubles function at first as projections of emotional obstacles to identity and then, in Viola and Sebastian, as the fulfillment of a wish for a way around the obstacles. The play abounds in images of engulfment and devouring connected with the sea and love; often it is suggested that love, like the sea, is boundless and voracious, swallowing up the lover. As John Hollander points out, the play is saturated in waters of various sorts, just as two of the main characters (and several of the minor ones) are suffused by their desires. Images of the sea (reinforced by allusions to ships, sailing, and sea-trading), of tears, rain, liquor, urine, and the humors appear frequently. First stated in Orsino's famous opening speech—

> O spirit of love, how quick and fresh art thou,
> That notwithstanding thy capacity
> Receiveth as the sea, nought enters there,
> Of what validity and pitch soe'er,
> But falls into abatement and low price,
> Even in a minute!
>
> (1.1.9–14)

From *Man's Estate: Masculine Identity in Shakespeare*. © 1981 by the Regents of the University of California. University of California Press, 1981.

—the idea is reiterated in the succeeding image of Orsino, like Actaeon, being torn apart by his desires. Though Orsino reverses the image in comparing his love to a woman's, saying,

> Alas, their love may be call'd appetite,
> No motion of the liver, but the palate,
> That suffers surfeit, cloyment, and revolt;
> But mine is all as hungry as the sea,
> And can digest as much,
>
> (2.4.98–102)

everything about him proclaims that it is he who is consumed by desire, and not the opposite. Skittish, giddy, "a very opal" of erotic whim, he himself is like the mutable sea. Similarly, when love comes stealing upon Olivia like the plague, her self-mortifying dedication to a dead brother vanishes instantly, and she becomes a bold wooer. When Orsino and Olivia love, they lose themselves in desire.

Interacting with this tendency to lose the self in surrender to eros, however, is the attempt to retain identity, through a narcissistic mirroring similar to that Antipholus S. sought in *Errors*, and through distancing oneself from the object of desire. Viola copes with the supposed loss of her twin brother by, in effect, becoming him; when she disguises herself as a man, she is another Sebastian, her twin's twin. Viola is paralleled and contrasted with Olivia, another grieving sister; "to season a brother's dead love" she vows to water her chamber once a day with tears. Sequestered with the memory of her brother, she rejects Orsino's constant suit and punishes the world by withdrawing her beauty from it. When Viola falls in love with Orsino, she devotes herself to a martyrdom similar to Olivia's. As long as her disguise proves convincing, she can never confess or consummate her love, and as Orsino's page, can only express it by furthering his suit to Olivia, her rival. Viola's disguise, it must be said, is to some extent necessitated by her circumstances, and unlike Olivia's attachment to her brother, is a conscious assumption of a different identity that she maintains in tandem with her real one. Both move, however, from loving dead brothers to loving unattainable male figures, maintaining a love whose distance does not threaten their persistent ties to the family through their brothers.

Orsino's love parallels theirs in the sense that his object is hopelessly unattainable, and in the exacerbated self-consciousness and distance it involves. His desire for Olivia can never be satisfied. Even though Orsino, like Olivia when she falls in love with Cesario, gives himself over to passion, that he chooses an unyielding object with whom real intimacy is impossible argues his fear of losing himself in passion.

Thus while all three characters fall madly in love, they all, in different ways, defend against eros as a threat to the integrity and stability of the self. It is the narcissistic mirroring in which Viola and Olivia engage, however, that is most relevant to the Shakespearean family romance. The twin and the sibling, for Viola and for Olivia, are versions of a need for primary ontological reassurance; like the mother, they are not fully differentiated from the self (they look the same, or similar, and are of the same blood) and thus they reaffirm the self at the most basic level, but keep it from developing further.

Mirroring is sought from a double of the opposite sex, however, which focuses the issue specifically on sexual identity rather than on identity per se as in *Errors*. The errors of *Twelfth Night* are not merely those of mistaken identity as in the earlier play, but errors that create an aura of doubt about the characters' sexual identity, for *us* rather than for them. *Twelfth Night* is frequently read as a play about masking, about the conscious and unconscious assumption of false identities and about levels of self-knowledge and self-deception; this theme is played out prominently through Viola's transsexual disguise.

For the greater part of the play, until act 5, scene 2, each of the three major characters is wholly certain of who it is that he or she loves: Orsino, unaware of his growing attachment to Cesario, ardently pursues Olivia; Olivia gives herself passionately to a man she knows as Cesario; and Viola is constant to Orsino. Viola's transsexual disguise, until she and Sebastian are mistaken for each other in the duel with Sir Andrew, works on us more deeply and disturbingly than it does on the characters it fools, precisely because it fools them and doesn't fool us. As we watch Viola mediating between Olivia and Orsino, inhabiting one sex with them and another with us, we are forced to conceive of novel and conflicting ways in which sexual identity might be detached from personal identity; we are cut loose from our habitual assumption that the two are inextricable, that the person is defined by his or her sex. In effect, we experience that state of radical identity-confusion typical of adolescence, when the differences between the sexes are as fluid as their desires for each other, when a boy might feel more like a girl than like a boy, or a girl might love another girl rather than a boy.

Consider these several possibilities. Olivia believes Cesario to be a man, but we know he is not and are titillated by the suggestion that Olivia, loving a woman instead of a man, is not the woman she should be. Similar doubts arise with Orsino, who has unclasped his bosom so readily to a charming boy. At the same time, Shakespeare lets us see that both Olivia and Orsino are drawn to Viola because they find in her those characteristics of the opposite sex to which they are attracted. Orsino says,

> For they shall yet belie thy happy years,
> That say thou art a man. Diana's lip
> Is not more smooth and rubious; thy small pipe
> Is as the maiden's organ, shrill and sound,
> And all is semblative a woman's part.
> I know thy constellation is right apt for this affair
>
> (1.4.30–35)

while Olivia, musing on Cesario's statement that he is "a gentleman," declares

> I'll be sworn thou art;
> Thy tongue, thy face, thy limbs, actions, and spirit
> Do give thee five-fold blazon. Not so fast: soft! soft!
> Unless the master were the man.
>
> (1.5.295–98)

At some level, Cesario is a homosexual object choice for each of them; at another, a heterosexual one. Yet "she" or "he" is the same person, one person. Creatures whose sexual identity is not simply and clearly male or female—hermaphrodites or eunuchs—threaten the binary opposition on which sexual identity, and much else in culture, is based. Without the strict differentiation of male from female, sexual integrity disappears and chaos impends. When Viola refers to herself as a "poor monster," she only touches on the fearsome aspects of her disguise that have been evident to us as she moves ambiguously from Orsino to Olivia.

Yet in the delicate comic irony of the scenes between Viola and each of the other two, Shakespeare reminds us through Viola's poignant double entendres of what Viola herself never forgets: that no matter how the duke and countess see her, she is not androgynous, but irreducibly a woman. The fluid sexual proclivities of youth promise to clash with the reality principle, for that "little thing" she thinks she lacks of being a man is crucial.

The early introduction of Sebastian into the play, however, assures us that all will end properly with a mate of the opposite sex for both Orsino and Olivia. When Sebastian and Viola recognize each other as brother and sister in the last scene, and Olivia is reprieved from the shadow of our doubt that she might have been in love with a woman, Sebastian says,

So comes it, lady, you have been mistook.
But nature to her bias drew in that.

(5.1.257–58)

Nature's bias is usually regarded as a heterosexual one, but the line is actually ambiguous; "nature's bias" can mean that Olivia followed nature in loving a woman, for a short and perhaps necessary period, before actually marrying a man. Similarly, Orsino perhaps needed to see Viola as a girlish boy before he could accept her as a real and ardent woman. The dramatic device of identical opposite-sex twins allows Orsino and Olivia to navigate the crucial passage from identification to object choice, from adolescent sexual experimentation to adult intimacy, from filial ties to adult independence, without even changing the object of their desires.

Feste's song, "When that I was and a little tiny boy," which concludes the play, states in its offhand, colloquial, cryptic way the conception of a man's life-cycle in terms of psychosexual stages that underlies the action of *Twelfth Night*. Several interpreters have suggested that the "foolish thing" of the first stanza is the *membrum virile*. Before the speaker comes to "man's estate," sexuality can be like a toy, playful and open to experimentation, fluid, spontaneous, and uncommitted; but man's "estate" in the second stanza implies status, responsibility, wealth, and property, which "knaves and thieves" may cheat him out of; he must leave sexual play behind, and in the third stanza, take himself a wife. Now the issue is "swaggering," the pretense and display of courtship, as we have seen it in the play through Orsino's elegant embassies of love and Sir Andrew's pathetic attempts at valor, neither of which "thrive." The song skips over marriage and parenthood, coming to rest in the puzzling fourth stanza at the last stage of life, a decline into drunkenness and sleep, before ending with a sigh at the perpetual recurrence of the cycle: "A great while ago the world began. . . . But that's all one, our play is done." *Twelfth Night* traces the evolution of sexuality as related to identity, from the playful and unconscious toyings of youthful courtship, through a period of sexual confusion, to a final thriving in which swaggering is left behind and men and women truly know themselves through choosing and loving the right mate.

Plays and Playing in *Twelfth Night*

Karen Greif

"The purpose of playing," says Hamlet, is "to hold as 'twere the mirror up to nature: to show virtue her feature, scorn her own image, and the very age and body of the time his form and pressure." Hamlet himself employs "playing," in various guises, as a means of penetrating false appearances to uncover hidden truths, but he also discovers how slippery illusions can be when their effects become entangled in the human world. Like *Hamlet*, but in a comic vein, *Twelfth Night* poses questions about "the purpose of playing" and about whether illusion is perhaps too deeply embedded in human experience to be ever completely separated from reality.

Virtually every character in *Twelfth Night* is either an agent or a victim of illusion, and often a player will assume both these roles: as Viola is an impostor but also a prisoner of her own disguise, or as Sir Toby loses control of the deception he has contrived when he mistakes Sebastian for his twin. Illyria is a world populated by pretenders, which has led one critic [Joseph H. Summers] to describe the action as "a dance of maskers . . . for the assumption of the play is that no one is without a mask in the serio-comic business of the pursuit of happiness." In the course of the story, many of these masks are stripped away or willingly set aside; but illusion itself plays a pivotal yet somewhat ambiguous role in this process. While Viola's masquerade serves to redeem Orsino and Olivia from their romantic fantasies and ends in happiness with the final love-matches, the more negative aspects of deception are exposed in the trick played against Malvolio, which leads only to humiliation and deeper isolation.

From *Shakespeare Survey: An Annual Survey of Shakespearean Study and Production*, volume 34, edited by Stanley Wells. © 1981 by Cambridge University Press.

Role-playing, deceptions, disguises, and comic manipulations provide the fabric of the entire action. So pervasive is the intermingling of illusion and reality in the play that it becomes impossible at times for the characters to distinguish between the two. This is not simply a case of illusion becoming a simulated version of reality. "I am not that I play," Viola warns her fellow player (1.5.184); but, as the subtitle suggests, in *Twelfth Night* one discovers that "what you will" may transform the ordinary shape of reality.

The fluidity of the relationship between "being" and "playing" is indirectly illuminated at the beginning of act 3, in the play's single face-to-face encounter between Viola and Feste, who share the distinction of being the only pretenders in Illyria who do not wear their motley in their brains. They match wits in a contest of wordplay, which moves the Fool to sermonize: "To see this age! A sentence is but a chev'ril glove to a good wit. How quickly the wrong side may be turn'd outward!" (3.1.11–13). According to Feste, words have become like kidskin gloves, pliable outside coverings readily yielding to manipulation by a good wit. Viola's response echoes this sense; those who know how to play with words "may quickly make them wanton" (15). Men may expect words to operate as constant symbols of meaning, faithfully reflecting the concrete outlines of reality; but, in fact, words prove to be flighty, untrustworthy mediators between human beings and experience:

> CLOWN. But indeed, words are very rascals since bonds
>   disgrac'd them.
> VIOLA. Thy reason, man?
> CLOWN. Troth, sir, I can yield you none without words, and
>   words are grown so false, I am loath to prove reason
>   with them.
>
> (3.1.20–25)

Rather than serving as a medium for straightforward communication, words have become bent to the purposes of dissembling. Feste declares himself a "corrupter of words" (36), and throughout the play he demonstrates how chameleon-like words can become in the mouth of an expert dissembler like himself. Yet Feste is also recognized by his audience and many of his fellow players as a kind of truth-teller; under the guise of fooling and ingenious word-play, he reminds those around him of truths they have blocked out of their illusion-bound existences. The Fool's dialogue with Viola suggests that "since bonds disgrac'd them," words have fallen under suspicion within the world of *Twelfth Night*, at least among those who admit their own dissembling. But for those who possess wit and imagination, the protean nature of words also affords an exhilarating form of release. Dexterity with language becomes a means of circumventing a world that is always shifting its outlines by exploiting that fluidity to the speaker's own advantage.

The same ambiguity that is characteristic of words pervades almost every aspect of human experience in *Twelfth Night*. Illyria is a world of deceptive surfaces, where appearances constantly fluctuate between what is real and what is illusory. Out of the sea, there comes into this unstable society a catalyst in the form of the disguised Viola, who becomes the agent required to free Orsino and Olivia from the bondage of their self-delusions. Equilibrium is finally attained, however, only after the presence of Viola and her separated twin has generated as much error and disturbance as Illyria could possibly contain.

Moreover, this resolution is achieved not by a straightforward injection of realism into this bemused dreamworld, but by further subterfuge. "Conceal me what I am," Viola entreats the Sea Captain after the shipwreck (1.2.53), setting in motion the twin themes of identity and disguise that motivate so much of the action in *Twelfth Night*. Identity, it is important to bear in mind, includes both the identity that represents the essence of one's being, the "what I am" that separates one individual from another, and also the identity that makes identical twins alike; and the comedy is concerned with the loss and the recovery of identity in both these senses.

Viola's plan to dissemble her true identity proves to be ironically in keeping with the milieu she has entered. But the fact that Viola, left stranded and unprotected by the wreck, assumes her guise as Cesario in response to a real predicament sets her apart from most of the pretenders already dwelling in Illyria. Surfeiting on fancy, they endlessly fabricate grounds for deceiving others or themselves. Orsino and Olivia are foolish, in part, because it is apparent that the roles of unrequited lover and grief-stricken lady they have chosen for themselves spring more from romantic conceits than from deep feeling or necessity. The games-playing mania of Sir Toby Belch and his cohorts carries to comic extremes the Illyrian penchant for playing make-believe. Just as words, in Sir Toby's hands, are rendered plastic by his Falstaffian talent for making their meaning suit his own convenience, so he manufactures circumstances to fit his will.

The kind of egotism that stamps Sir Toby's perpetual manipulation of words and appearances, or Orsino and Olivia's wilful insistence on their own way, is far removed from Viola's humility as a role-player. Although she shares Feste's zest for wordplay and improvisation, Viola never deludes herself into believing she has absolute control over either her own part or the actions of her fellow players. Musing over the complications of the love triangle into which her masculine disguise has thrust her, Viola wryly concedes "O time, thou must untangle this, not I, / It is too hard a knot for me t'untie" (2.2.40–41). Viola's outlook is unaffectedly realistic without the need to reject imaginative possibilities. Her own miraculous escape encourages her to hope her brother has also survived the wreck, but throughout most of the play she must continue to act without any certainty he is still alive. She accepts the facts of her dilemma without self-pity and begins at once to improvise a new, more flexible role for herself in a difficult situation; but she also learns that the freedom playing permits her is only a circumscribed liberty. For as long as the role of Cesario conceals her real identity, Viola is free to move at will through Illyria, but not to reveal her true nature or her love for Orsino.

The first meeting between Cesario and Olivia creates one of the most demanding tests of Viola's ability to improvise. She meets the challenge with ingenuity, but Viola also insists, with deliberate theatricality, on the disparity between her true self and the role that she dissembles:

> VIOLA. I can say little more than I have studied, and that
> question's out of my part. Good gentle one, give me
> modest assurance if you be the lady of the house, that I
> may proceed in my speech.
> OLIVIA. Are you a comedian?
> VIOLA. No, my profound heart; and yet (by the very fangs of
> malice I swear) I am not that I play.
>
> (1.5.178–84)

In her exchanges with Olivia, Viola is able to treat the part she plays with comic detachment; but the somewhat rueful tone underlying her awareness of the ironies of her relation to Olivia turns to genuine heartache when this separation between her true identity and her assumed one comes into conflict with her growing love for Orsino.

Unable to reveal her love openly, Viola conjures for Orsino the imaginary history of a sister who

> lov'd a man
> As it might be perhaps, were I a woman,
> I should your lordship.
>
> (2.4.107–9)

As long as Orsino clings to his fancied passion for Olivia and she herself holds on to her disguise, Viola can vent her true feelings only by more dissembling, so she masks her secret love for the Duke with the sad tale of this lovelorn sister. Yet her fiction also serves to present her master with a portrait of genuine love against which to measure his own obsession for Olivia. "Was this not love indeed?" she challenges him:

> We men may say more, swear more, but indeed
> Our shows are more than will; for still we prove
> Much in our vows, but little in our love.
>
> (2.4.116–18)

Her story is a touching one, and for once Orsino's blustering is stilled. He is moved to wonder "But died thy sister of her love, my boy?"; but she offers only the cryptic answer "I am all the daughters of my father's house, / And all the brothers too—and yet I know not" (119–21). Viola's veiled avowal of her love is perhaps the most delicate blend of imagination and truth in the play, and this fabrication will finally yield its reward when Cesario is free to disclose "That I am Viola" (5.1.253).

Role-playing, whether it be a deliberate choice like Viola's disguise or the foolish self-delusions that Orsino, Olivia, and Malvolio all practise upon themselves, leads to a general confusion of identity within Illyria. In the second encounter between Olivia and Cesario, this tension between being and playing is given special resonance:

> OLIVIA. I prithee tell me what thou think'st of me.
> VIOLA. That you do think you are not what you are.
> OLIVIA. If I think so, I think the same of you.
> VIOLA. Then think you right: I am not what I am.
> OLIVIA. I would you were as I would have you be.
> VIOLA. Would it be better, madam, than I am?
>   I wish it might, for now I am your fool.
>
> (3.1.138–44)

Like a tonic chord in a musical passage, Viola's riddles always come back to the idea of "what you are" and "what I am," the enduring truth of one's real identity. But this note of resolution is never a stable one. Viola warns Olivia that she has deluded herself into acting out fantasies with no basis in reality, first in her vow of celibacy to preserve her grief and then in her pursuit of the unattainable Cesario. In turn, she herself admits that "I am not what I am." Olivia, meanwhile, is obsessed with "what thou think'st of me" and what "I would have you be." She is less interested in the truth about Cesario or her own nature than in making what is conform to what she would like it to be. On the one hand, the facts of nature ensure that she will be frustrated in her wooing, and yet her beloved will indeed be transformed into what she would have him be when the counterfeit Cesario is replaced by the real Sebastian.

The compression of so many levels of meaning within this passage suggests how complicated and paradoxical the relationship is in *Twelfth Night* between what actually is and what playing with reality can create. Viola's exchange with Olivia follows directly upon her encounter with Feste, and the second dialogue translates into terms of identity and role-playing the same attitudes towards words appearing in the first. The Fool claims that "since bonds disgrac'd them," words have no static nature— that no unchanging identification between the-thing-itself and the word symbolizing it is ever possible—and the condition of being, the identity belonging to "what I am," is in a comparable state of flux throughout most of the action.

The separation between being and playing, like the disjunction be-tween words and concrete reality, may lead to a sense of disorientation closely akin to madness. This is the condition that the release of imagination creates in Malvolio. When he exchanges the reality of what he is for the make-believe part he dreams of becoming, he begins to act like a madman. Viola's charade as Cesario produces a welter of mistaken identities that so disorient her fellow players no one is quite certain of his or her sanity. Yet another variation of the madness which springs from unleashing the effects of imagination upon reality is seen in the escapades of Sir Toby Belch. His reign of misrule is fuelled by his refusal to allow reality to interfere with his desires, and this unruliness drives his associates to wonder repeatedly if he is mad.

Yet, just as Feste finds means of communicating truth by playing with words, so does the unstable relationship between being and playing allow at least a few of the players in Illyria to discover a more flexible sense of identity that can accommodate both enduring truths and changing appearances. The same loosening of the bonds governing identity that can lead to bewildering confusion may also open up a fresh sense of freedom in shaping one's own nature. What you will may indeed transform what you are.

The point at which all these attitudes converge is in the recognition scene of the final act. At the moment when Viola and Sebastian finally come face to face upon the stage, the climactic note of this motif is sounded in Orsino's exclamation of wonder:

> One face, one voice, one habit, and two persons,
> A natural perspective, that is and is not!
>
> (5.1.216–17)

For the onlookers, who are still ignorant both of Viola's true identity and of the existence of her twin, the mirror image created by the twins' confrontation seems explicable only as an optical illusion of nature. Yet the illusion proves to be real; this "natural perspective" is the stable reality underlying the mirage of shifting appearances caused by mistaken identity.

This dramatic revelation of the identity that has been obscured by illusory appearances, but is now made visible in the mirror image of the twins, is deliberately prolonged as Viola and Sebastian exchange their tokens of recognition. Anne Barton has drawn attention to the fact that the recognition scene provides

> a happy ending of an extraordinarily schematized and "playlike" kind. Viola has already had virtual proof, in act 3, that her brother has survived the wreck. They have been separated for only three months. Yet the two of them put each other through a formal, intensely conventional question and answer test that comes straight out of Greek New Comedy.

The recognition of identity is at first an experience involving only the reunited twins; but, as the facts of their kinship are brought forth, the circle of awareness expands to include Orsino and Olivia. They appreciate for the first time their shared folly in desiring the unobtainable and both discover true love in unexpected forms by sharing in the recognition of the twins' identities. As Orsino vows,

> If this be so, as yet the glass seems true,
> I shall have share in this most happy wrack.
> (5.1.265–66)

The reflections of identity that have been present throughout the play are now openly acknowledged and sealed by the bonds of marriage and kinship. The similarities between Viola and Olivia, for example—the lost brother, the unrequited love, the veiled identity—which are echoed in the names that are virtually anagrams, are now confirmed by the ties of sisterhood when each wins the husband she desires.

Paradoxically, what allows this dramatic moment of epiphany to occur at all is the same loss and mistaking of identities that caused the original confusion. It is the separation of the twins and Viola's subsequent decision to "Conceal me what I am" which gives emotional intensity to the moment when identity is recognized and regained. This final scene, moreover, makes it clear that the regaining of lost personal identity—the individuality that distinguishes Viola from Sebastian—is closely tied to the recognition of the likeness that makes the twins identical. The recognition scene, with its ritual-like ceremony of identification, suggests that men and women must recognize how much they are identical, how much alike in virtues and follies and in experiences and desires, before they can affirm the personal identities that make them unique. These twin senses of identity converge in the final act, dramatically embodied in the reunited twins who share "One face, one voice, one habit, and two persons."

But at what point do the reflections stop? Beyond the onlookers upon the stage who behold this ceremony of recognition is the larger audience of the illusion that is *Twelfth Night*. The play itself is "a natural perspective, that is and is not": a mirror held up to nature intended to reflect the contours of reality and simultaneously a work of imagination that incarnates the world of being in a world of playing. What the audience encounters in the mirror of the play is its own reflected identity in the characters who play out their experiences upon the stage. In sharing the experience of *Twelfth Night*, we come to recognize the ties of identity that link our own world of being to the imagined world of the play; and, on a more personal level, we identify our private follies and desires in our fictional counterparts upon the stage. In acknowledging this kinship of resemblance, we too gain a fresh awareness of the nature of "what I am," the true self concealed beneath the surface level of appearances. Moreover, having witnessed how deeply life is ingrained with illusion within Illyria, we may awake from the dreamworld of the play to wonder if "what we are" in the world outside the playhouse is perhaps less static and immutable than we once believed. At this point, imagination and truth may begin to merge in our own world: "Prove true, imagination, O, prove true" (3.4.375).

If art possesses this creative power, however, there remains the·problem of dealing with the more troubling issues raised by the gulling of Malvolio. The plot contrived to convince the steward of Olivia's passion for him is enacted with deliberately theatrical overtones, and the conspirators employ deception to feed and then expose Malvolio's folly in much the same way that a playwright manipulates illusion and reality upon the stage. Yet Malvolio's enforced immersion in the world of make-believe in no way reforms him. Nor does it enable him to gain a more positive understanding of either his own identity or the ties that bind him to his fellow men. Malvolio remains isolated and egotistical to the end. What is more, the mockers who have seen their own follies reflected in Malvolio's comic performance are no more altered by the experience than he is.

The plot against Malvolio is originally planned along the traditional lines of Jonsonian "humour" comedy: the victim's folly is to be exposed and purged by comic ridicule to rid him of his humour. Maria explains the scheme in such terms to her fellow satirists

> it is his grounds of faith that all that look on him love
> him; and on that vice in him will my revenge find notable cause
> to work. . . . I know my physic will work with him.
>
> (2.3.151–53, 172–73)

But there is also a strong dose of personal spite in their mockery. The pranksters are really more eager to be entertained by Malvolio's delusions of grandeur than they are to reform him. Maria guarantees her audience that "If I do not gull him into an ayword, and make him a common recreation, do not think I have wit enough to lie straight in my bed" (134–37). It is certainly in this spirit that the revellers take the jest. "If I lose a scruple of this sport," Fabian pledges as the game begins, "let me be boil'd to death with melancholy" (2.5.2–3).

Maria plants the conspirators in the garden box-tree like spectators at a play, bidding them: "Observe him, for the love of mockery; for I know this letter will make a contemplative idiot of him" (18–20). Malvolio, who "has been yonder i' the sun practising behavior to his own shadow this half hour" (16–18), is a natural play-actor; and he immediately takes the bait of this improvised comedy. The megalomania suppressed beneath his Puritan facade is comically set free by the discovery of Maria's forged letter, and he is soon persuaded to parade his folly publicly by donning the famous yellow stockings.

Maria's letter cleverly exploits Mavolio's conceit, but he himself manufactures his obsession. With only the flimsiest of clues to lead him on, Malvolio systematically construes every detail of the letter to fuel his newly liberated dreams of greatness, never pausing to consider how ludicrous the message really is:

> Why, this is evident to any formal capacity, there is no obstruc-
> tion in this. And the end—what should that alphabetical posi-
> tion portend? If I could make that resemble something in
> me! . . . M.O.A.I. This simulation is not as the former; and yet,
> to crush this a little, it would bow to me, for every one of these
> letters are in my name.
>
> (116–20, 139–41)

The deception deftly juggles appearances to prompt Malvolio to his own undoing, but there is always the danger inherent in such games of make-believe that the dupe will no longer be able to cope with reality once his self-fabricated fantasies are stripped away from him. "Why, thou hast put him in such a dream," Sir Toby laughingly tells Maria, "that when the image of it leaves him he must run mad" (193–94). But no such qualms disturb these puppet-masters. When Fabian echoes this warning, Maria replies "The house will be the quieter" (3.4.134).

Although it is the letter that persuades Malvolio to play out his fantasies in public, his audience has already been treated to a display of his fondness for make-believe. While the conspirators impatiently wait for him to stumble on the letter, Malvolio muses on his dream of becoming the rich and powerful "Count Malvolio." As he paints the imaginary scene of Sir Toby's future humiliation and expulsion, the eavesdroppers find themselves unexpectedly drawn into the performance they are watching. Sir Toby, in particular, becomes so enraged at this "overweening rogue" (29) that Fabian must repeatedly warn him to control his outbursts: "Nay, patience, or we break the sinews of our plot!" (75–76). Malvolio's audience prove to be as uncertain as their gull about the boundaries separating fiction from fact, as will be made comically evident in the miscalculations and confusions that result from the duel contrived between Sir Andrew and Cesario. Taken unawares by Malvolio's tableau of future triumph, the three spies inadvertently become participants in the comedy they are observing.

Malvolio's private playlet of revenge and his discovery of the letter are staged in a deliberately theatrical manner, played before the unruly audience of Sir Toby, Sir Andrew, and Fabian. His play-acting exposes Malvolio's folly to comic perfection; but it also, in its own topsy-turvy fashion, holds the mirror up to nature for both the spectators in the box-tree and the audience beyond the stage. It is a glass more like a funhouse mirror than the symmetry of a "natural perspective," but in Malvolio's absurd performance the pranksters are presented with a comically distorted image of their own follies and delusions. Malvolio's folly is made more ludicrous by the charade that openly exposes the overweening ambition and conceit normally held within respectable bounds by the sanctimonious steward, but the difference between the performer and his audience is simply one of degree.

If Malvolio is treated by these practical jokers as a puppet on a string, a "trout that must be caught with tickling" (2.5.22), Sir Andrew is no less Sir Toby's own "dear manikin" (3.2.53). His auditors deride Malvolio's pretensions to his mistress's love; but Sir Andrew's wooing of Olivia is equally preposterous, and his hopes are based entirely on Sir Toby's counterfeit assurances. Sir Toby may ridicule Malvolio's determined efforts to "crush" the letter's message to accommodate his own desires, but the assertion of imagination over concrete reality is no less a characteristic trait of Sir Toby himself, who has earlier insisted that "Not to be a-bed after midnight is to be up betimes" (2.3.1–2). The only difference in their dealings with words is that Malvolio uses logic as a crowbar to twist and hammer meanings into a more gratifying form, while Sir Toby chooses to suspend logic altogether.

The steward's obsessive instinct for order is simply the inverted image of Sir Toby's own mania for disorder. Even their plot to put an end to Malvolio's authority is dramatized for the spectators in a parody version supplied by Malvolio's own dream of revenge.

The spectators are in their own ways as much drowned in excesses of folly and imagination as their gull. But as they mock the woodcock nearing the gin, the onlookers fail to realize that the "play" itself is an imaginary snare for the woodcocks in its audience. Sir Andrew's reaction to Malvolio's fictive dialogue with a humbled Sir Toby exemplifies the fatuity of his fellow auditors:

> MALVOLIO. "Besides, you waste the treasure of your time with
>   a foolish knight"—
> ANDREW. That's me, I warrant you.
> MALVOLIO. "One Sir Andrew"—
> ANDREW. I knew 'twas I, for many do call me fool.
>
> (2.5.77–81)

Sir Andrew makes the correct identification but remains oblivious to the intended reprimand. In the same fashion, all the members of Malvolio's audience observe their reflected images in the mirror of the comedy without recognition, thus comically fulfilling Jonathan Swift's famous dictum that "Satyr is a sort of Glass, wherein Beholders do generally discover every body's Face but their own."

By the time Malvolio encounters Olivia again after reading her supposed declaration of love, his perceptions have become completely mastered by his delusions. To those around him who are unaware of the deception, Malvolio appears quite mad. "Why, this is very midsummer madness," (3.4.56) cries Olivia in response to the incoherent ramblings of this smiling, cross-gartered apparition. From his own perspective, however, he is unquestionably sane, and it is the rest of the world that is behaving strangely. Unlike Viola or Feste, Malvolio has no talent for improvisation. His rejection of a rigidly defined identity, although it gives him a temporary release from social bonds, affords Malvolio no room for flexibility.

Faced with the fluidity of the world of playing in which he suddenly finds himself, Malvolio insists on trying to marshal shifting appearances back into regimented formation:

> Why, every thing adheres together, that no dram of a scruple,
>   no scruple of a scruple, no obstacle, no incredulous or unsafe
>   circumstance—What can be said?
>
> (3.4.78–81)

But Malvolio's efforts to control the flux are like trying to sculpt water into solid shapes; the material itself refuses static form. His obstinate insistence that the words and actions of those around him should conform to his will makes him appear mad to his fellow players, while they seem equally insane to him.

The quandary over who is mad and who is sane becomes even more entangled in the dialogue between the incarcerated steward and the Fool, disguised as Sir Topas. Malvolio is entirely just in his charge that "never was man thus wrong'd. . . . They have laid me here in hideous darkness" (4.2.28–30). From his perspective, the darkness is tangible and his madness the fantasy of those around him. Yet it is also true, as "Sir Topas" insists, that the darkness is symbolic of the shroud of ignorance and vanity through which Malvolio views the world:

> MALVOLIO. I am not mad, Sir Topas, I say to you this house is
> dark.
> CLOWN. Madman, thou errest. I say there is no darkness but
> ignorance, in which thou art more puzzled than the
> Egyptians in their fog.
> MALVOLIO. I say this house is as dark as ignorance, though
> ignorance were as dark as hell; and I say there was never
> man thus abus'd. I am no more mad than you are.
>
> (4.2.40–48)

His "confessor's" riddles seem designed to force Malvolio to a new understanding of his identity as a fallible and often foolish human being. But "Sir Topas" is himself a fake—a self-avowed corrupter of words whose disguised purpose is not to heal Malvolio's imagined lunacy, but to drive him deeper into madness. Feste juggles words with ease because he understands that they are "very rascals since bonds disgrac'd them," but Malvolio stubbornly insists on making rascal words behave with as much decorum as he believes they should. Throughout this scene, Malvolio returns to his claim "I am not mad" with the same tonic emphasis as Viola reverts to "what I am" in her dialogue with Olivia (act 3, scene 1). But being incapable of Viola's playful attitude, Malvolio rejects any imaginative interpretation of his dilemma.

His rigidity toward both language and experience leaves him incapable of comprehending any truth beyond the concrete limits of reality. "I tell thee I am as well in my wits as any man in Illyria" (4.2.106–7), Malvolio insists with absolute justice; but how far from madness are the other inhabitants of Illyria? In a very ironic sense, Malvolio gets what he deserves when he is imprisoned in his cell. Having persisted in imposing his arbitrary order upon capricious words and appearances, he is himself confined in a guard-house for his own caprices.

Whatever his deserts, there is nonetheless considerable justice to Mal-volio's charge that he has been much abused by the deceivers who have made him "the most notorious geck and gull / That e'er invention play'd on" (5.1.343–44). Ironically, Malvolio's absurdly inflated ego and his isola-tion are only hardened by his satiric treatment. Even in making his defence, Malvolio stubbornly maintains yet another delusion, that Olivia is person-ally responsible for his torment. Humiliated beyond endurance, Malvolio stalks off the stage with a final ringing assertion of his vanity and alienation: "I'll be reveng'd on the whole pack of you" (378). Malvolio stands as an isolated figure in a festive world from beginning to end because never once does he honestly perceive his own nature, the true identity of "what I am," or the corresponding ties of identity that bind him to his fellow players.

The pranksters, in spite of their fondness for "fellowship," do not fare much better. They have already demonstrated a failure to detect their own follies in Malvolio's pretensions, and it is therefore appropriate that the beguilers as well as their gull should be missing from the witnesses at the recognition scene and the subsequent revelations. Sir Toby, in particular, suffers for his failures of identification. After having challenged Sebastian to a fight in the mistaken belief he was the timorous Cesario, Sir Toby rages onto the stage with a bloody head, angrily spurning the comfort of his friend Sir Andrew: "Will you help?—an ass-head and a coxcomb and a knave, a thin-fac'd knave, a gull!" (5.1.206–7).

Whereas the mistaken identities and role-playing in the romantic plot centring on Viola ultimately lead, in the recognition scene, to a renewal of identity and the human bonds of kinship and marriage, Malvolio's immer-sion in a world of make-believe yields no such beneficial rewards. The ironic counterpart to the recognition scene with its unravelling of identities is Malvolio's dungeon scene. There, Malvolio is literally enclosed in dark-ness in a cell cutting him off from all direct human contact, and he is bedevilled by tricksters who would like to drive him into deeper confusion. Nor does his audience there or in the garden scene gain any greater insight into their own characters. This failure of imagination, set against Viola's own miraculous success, reflects ironically on the supposedly therapeutic value of "playing" and the dubious morality of the would-be satirists as much as it does on Malvolio's own recalcitrance. Malvolio's final words and his incensed departure add a discordant note to the gracefully orchestrated harmonies of the final act.

Malvolio's response to his comic purgatory stirs unresolved questions about the value of playing with reality. Whereas Viola's part in the comedy reveals how the release that playing allows can lead to a renewed sense of identity and human bonds, Malvolio's role exposes the other side of the coin, the realm in which release of imagination leads only to greater isolation and imperception. Fabian's jest about Malvolio's absurd play-acting, "If this were play'd upon a stage now, I could condemn it as an improbable fiction" (3.4.127–28), like the theatrical overtones of Viola's improvisations and the playlike quality of the recognition scene, deliberately opens up the vistas of the play by reminding us that we are witnesses of a play, "a natural perspective, that is and is not." But amusing as Malvolio's surrender to playing is, it raises the most disturbing questions in the play. Can men, in fact, ever perfectly distinguish what is real from what is imagined or intentionally spurious? Can they ever come to know the truth about themselves, the identity appearances have concealed from them?

Twelfth Night itself offers no pat solutions. In a comic world devoted to playing and yet mirroring the actual world of being, in which identities are both mistaken and revealed, in which deception can both conceal truths and expose them, and in which bonds have disgraced the words on which men are dependent for communication, no permanent resolution of these ambiguities is ever possible. Shakespeare himself shrugs off the task of providing any final illumination with delightful finesse. As the play draws to a close with Feste's epilogue song and the world of playing begins to dissolve back into the world of being, the Fool concludes:

> A great while ago the world begun,
>   With hey ho, the wind and the rain,
> But that's all one, our play is done,
>   And we'll strive to please you every day.

The Principle of Recompense in *Twelfth Night*

Camille Slights

Like Shakespeare's other romantic comedies, *Twelfth Night* moves from personal frustration and social disorder to individual fulfilment and social harmony by means of what Leo Salingar has shown to be the traditional comic combination of beneficent fortune and human intrigue. This basic pattern, of course, takes a radically different form in each play. In comparison with many of the comedies, *Twelfth Night* begins with remarkably little conflict. The opening scenes introduce no villain bent on dissension and destruction, nor do they reveal disruptive antagonism between parents and children or between love and law. In contrast to the passion and anger of the first scene of *A Midsummer Night's Dream*, the restless melancholy that pervades the beginning of *The Merchant of Venice*, or the brutality and tyranny that precipitate the action in *As You Like It*, the dominant note of Orsino's court and of Olivia's household is static self-containment. To be sure, both Orsino and Olivia sincerely profess great unhappiness, but, as many critics have noted, a strain of complacent self-absorption dilutes the poignancy of Orsino's love-melancholy and of Olivia's grief. Orsino's concentration on his own emotions cuts him off from real personal relationships as effectively as does Olivia's withdrawal or Sir Toby's careless hedonism. The self-absorption of the native Illyrians and Viola's involuntary exile present a spectacle of isolation rather than confrontation, not so much a society in disorder as a series of discrete individuals without the interconnexions that constitute a society.

From *Modern Language Review* 77, no. 3 (July 1982). © 1982 by the Modern Humanities Research Association.

While the beginning of *Twelfth Night* is unusually static, the conclusion is strikingly active. Far from tying up a few loose ends, the last scene contains major events in both the double main plot and the sub-plot. Both pairs of lovers meet with full awareness for the first time. Viola finally wins Orsino's love, Orsino and Olivia, in different ways, discover whom it is they love, and Malvolio is released from imprisonment. Beginning calmly and purposefully enough with Orsino's first attempt to woo Olivia in person, the scene gathers intensity through a series of increasingly bitter confrontations. Orsino's banter with Feste is interrupted when Antonio appears, ominously under armed guard. Recognition as the duke's old enemy, however, is less galling to him than the apparent ingratitude of Sebastian (Viola-Cesario). At Olivia's entrance the tone darkens further with Orsino's jealous spite and threat to murder his presumed rival, to "sacrifice the lamb that I do love" (5.1.130). On the priest's confirming Cesario's marriage to Olivia, Orsino's rage is replaced by even more bitter contempt at such betrayal. In quick succession Viola-Cesario has provoked condemnation as an "ingrateful boy" (77) from Antonio, sorrow at the faithless cowardice of her new husband from Olivia, and, from the man she loves, a threat of death and disgusted rejection as "a dissembling cub" (164). The crescendo of pain and anger climaxes in the bloody spectacle of Sir Andrew's and Sir Toby's broken heads and Toby's vicious attack on his friend: "Will you help?—an ass-head and a coxcomb and a knave, a thin-fac'd knave, a gull!" (206).

At the midpoint of the scene, as Sir Toby and Sir Andrew exit to find help for their bleeding heads, Sebastian enters and the scene reverses direction. In the first half, relationships disintegrate in the whirling confusions of mistaken identities emanating from Viola's disguise. In the second half, new relationships form from the revelation and identification of the twins, Sebastian and Viola. The scene performs the conventional function of uniting lovers and reuniting family, but the emphasis is less on restoration and reconciliation than on the discovery of unexpected relationships and acceptance of new obligations. Sebastian's reunions with Antonio and Viola reveal that Olivia is betrothed not to a cowardly faithless boy but to a strong loyal man. By identifying Viola, Sebastian's appearance transforms Orsino from Cesario's master and Olivia's unsuccessful suitor into Viola's future husband and Olivia's prospective brother-in-law. Viola suddenly hears herself hailed as Olivia's sister and Orsino's mistress. Through marriages prospective and already performed, Maria, Toby, Olivia, Sebastian, Viola, and Orsino become one extended family, in households where Malvolio, Fabian, and Feste have secure positions.

In *Twelfth Night*, then, the comic movement from disorder to harmony is more particularly the transformation of isolation and fragmentation into mutuality and cohesion. The personal and societal problems at the beginning of the play result not from envy, aggression, or malice, but from a perhaps no less insidious, and equally universal, ambition for self-sufficiency. As the social anthropologist Claude Lévi-Strauss points out,

> mankind has always dreamed of seizing and fixing that fleeting moment when it was permissible to believe that the law of exchange could be evaded, that one could gain without losing, enjoy without sharing. At either end of the earth and at both extremes of time, the Sumerian myth of the golden age and the Andaman myth of the future life correspond, . . . removing to an equally unattainable past or future the joys, eternally denied to social man, of a world in which one might *keep to oneself.*
>
> (*The Elementary Structures of Kinship*)

Orsino's vision of self-surfeiting desires, Olivia's projected isolation, Toby's life of unconfined pleasure, and Malvolio's "practicing behavior to his own shadow" (2.5.17) are all versions of this dream of inviolable autonomy. Their various attempts to create these solipsistic paradises in Illyria produce an atmosphere of sterility, a society without cohesion. While a current of self-indulgence runs through Orsino's and Olivia's pain, the real dangers of isolation from the protection of human society threaten the more cheerful characters. Viola and Sebastian are separated and shipwrecked in unknown country, Sir Toby and Feste are threatened with dismissal from Olivia's household, and Antonio is banned from Orsino's territory on pain of death. By the end of the play this sense of incipient disintegration has disappeared from the enlarged and cohesive group, and the communal joy and affection are achieved largely in terms of what Lévi-Strauss, in the passage quoted above, calls the law of exchange.

Instead of celebrating personal and social harmony with the dancing and wedding festivities that end most of the comedies, the final scene of *Twelfth Night* demonstrates the mutual obligations imposed by the complicated new relationships. Public recognition of Viola's female identity depends on recovering her "maid's garments" (275) from the sea captain who befriended her. The captain, in prison under some legal obligation to Malvolio, cannot be released until Malvolio is satisfied. The need for Malvolio reminds Olivia of her responsibility to him and Feste of the letter in his charge. The letter brings Malvolio's release, which in turn precipitates Fabian's confession of responsibility. Meanwhile Olivia's and Sebastian's wedding festivities wait on Orsino's and Viola's, and Viola remains Cesario until Malvolio is pacified. This cycle of mutual dependence gives an open-ended quality to the ending of the play. Our confident expectation that "golden time" (382) will bring happiness to the lovers is complemented by our sense of continuing obligations. Reciprocal love, the design of *Twelfth Night* implies, naturally culminates not in a private dream-world of complete fulfilment, but in the give and take of human society.

This happy, albeit imperfect, ending is possible only when the major characters have come to terms with the inescapable mutuality of communal life through a series of exchanges, often financial transactions. We usually think of *The Merchant of Venice* as Shakespeare's treatment of the relationship of wealth to love, but, as Porter Williams, Jr., has pointed out, "seldom in a play does money flow so freely" as in *Twelfth Night*. Viola gives gold to the sea captain, Antonio gives his purse to Sebastian, Orsino sends a jewel to Olivia, Olivia showers gifts on Cesario, Viola-Cesario offers to divide her wealth with Antonio, and they all repeatedly give money to Feste. Economic advantage is not a prime motive for any of the characters, but hardly a scene goes by when they are not engaged in giving or receiving money or jewels. The lovers in the forest of Arden may rely on Hymen to arrange their nuptials, but in Illyria Olivia knows that someone must pay for the double wedding that is to replace the differences and frustrations of the past with a joyous alliance:

> My lord, so please you, these things further thought on,
> To think me as well a sister as a wife,
> One day shall crown th'alliance on't, so please you,
> Here at my house and at my proper cost.
>
> (5.1.316)

Illyria definitely is not Gonzalo's imaginary commonwealth without trade, service, or riches.

This emphasis on giving and receiving serves, as Porter Williams says, to contrast the generous and loving nature of Viola, Orsino, and Olivia with the selfishness of Malvolio and Sir Toby, but he oversimplifies, I think, when he suggests that the money and gifts that change hands so freely "symbolize generous love and friendship" and that "such giving and receiving must be done without counting the cost or measuring the risk." Orsino's financial generosity is patently not identified with generous love. Admittedly, he does not count the cost in his courtship of Olivia. His motives are not mercenary and his emissaries bear jewels; nevertheless, his love is self-regarding. In the first scene, for example, when he makes the expected pun on Curio's suggestion to hunt the hart, he first seems to be directing his thoughts beyond himself, thinking of the noble Olivia:

> CURIO. Will you go hunt, my lord?
> DUKE.   What, Curio?
> CURIO.   The hart.
> DUKE. Why, so I do, the noblest that I have.
>
> (1.1.16)

But immediately we discover that the noble heart Orsino pursues is his own:

> O, when mine eyes did see Olivia first,
> Methought she purg'd the air of pestilence!
> That instant was I turn'd into a hart,
> And my desires, like fell and cruel hounds,
> E'er since pursue me.
>
> (1.1.18)

His love for Olivia does not give rise to thoughts of serving her or sharing with her but of reigning supreme in her

>   when liver, brain, and heart,
> These sovereign thrones, are all supplied and fill'd
> Her sweet perfections with one self king!
>
> (1.1.36)

In the meantime he seeks solitude: "for I myself am best / When least in company" (1.4.37).

Viola too is generous, but, while her love is more selfless than Orsino's, her economic liberality is less purely spontaneous and more thoughtful. When she gives gold to the sea captain, she does so explicitly in gratitude for the comfort he has given her: "For saying so, there's gold" (1.2.18). She promises to pay him more in return for specific help she requests from him:

> I prithee (and I'll pay thee bounteously)
> Conceal me what I am, and be my aid
> For such disguise as haply shall become
> The form of my intent.
>
> (1.2.52)

She is fully aware that she takes a risk in trusting him:

> And though that nature with a beauteous wall
> Doth oft close in pollution, yet of thee
> I will believe thou hast a mind that suits
> With this thy fair and outward character.
>
> (1.2.48)

And she is not averse to reinforcing his good will with the hope that "It may be worth thy pains" (57). Just as she gladly pays for help she needs, she expects to earn her way with the duke she proposes to serve, confident that she can prove "worth his service" (59). Like the other characters, Viola is tempted by the attractions of solitude: she would like to join Olivia in her isolated grief and postpone being "delivered to the world" (42), but she readily accepts the necessity of taking part in the commerce of human society.

The idea of reward for service continues in Viola's first scene with Orsino. The short scene opens with Valentine commenting on Cesario's advancement: "If the Duke continue these favors towards you, Cesario, you are like to be much advanc'd; he hath known you but three days, and already you are no stranger" (4). The dialogue between Orsino and Viola ends with the duke's promise:

> Prosper well in this,
> And thou shalt live as freely as thy lord,
> To call his fortunes thine.
>
> (1.4.38)

The effect is not to stress Orsino's generosity, or to suggest his vulgarity in offering reward, but to show that Viola belongs; she has become an active participant in the reciprocal relationships that bind the social group together. Indeed, the play as a whole, I think, demonstrates the principle of reciprocity, the unwritten rule, according to Marcel Mauss and Lévi-Strauss, by which the exchange of goods creates mutually satisfying relationships among individuals and groups.

Building on Mauss's seminal study of the gift in primitive societies, these social anthropologists point out that exchanges of goods may be complex social events—at once legal, economic, religious, aesthetic, and morphological—rather than solely, or even primarily, economic transactions. Most basically, "the agreed transfer of a valuable from one individual to another makes these individuals into partners" because it implies that the gift will be reciprocated with a counter-gift, usually of equivalent or greater value. Through the principle of reciprocity, then, the art of exchange binds the giver and the recipient in a relationship. To give is to create an obligation; to take is to imply a willingness to pay that debt. Consequently, to refuse a gift is an insulting rejection of relationship with the giver, and to take without repaying is either humiliating failure or an act of aggression in the eyes of the whole society.

The principle of reciprocity operates most clearly through Feste. His first scene, act 1, scene 5, establishes his position as a professional entertainer. After Maria's warning that his absence has threatened his security as Olivia's fool, he successfully fools Olivia out of her bad humour and in return receives her support and protection when Malvolio attacks him. In act 2 he sings, first for Sir Toby and Sir Andrew, and then for Orsino, demonstrating each time that he who pays the piper calls the tune. There is nothing demeaning in the financial aspect of the transaction, despite A. C. Bradley's worry that Feste is offended and disgusted by Orsino's offer of payment. Feste sings for pleasure, as he tells Orsino, but "pleasure will be paid, one time or another" (2.4.70), and he pockets as his due the money Toby, Andrew, and Orsino pay for the pleasure he gives them. The scenes where Feste is paid for his foolery follow the same pattern. In act 3, scene 1, his witty wordplays elicit coins from Viola as well as an appreciative analysis of the fool's art. Similarly, at the beginning of act 5, scene 1, Orsino pays for Feste's excellent foolery and promises further bounty if he will carry a message. Feste's cleverness in getting his tips doubled, as he tells Orsino, is not "the sin of covetousness" (5.1.47), but part of his performance, rather like the plea for applause by the epilogue to a Renaissance play. Often, Feste expresses gratitude for these payments in a wittily pertinent blessing: "Now the melancholy good protect thee" to Orsino, and to Viola-Cesario: "Now Jove, in his next commodity of hair, send thee a beard!" (2.4.73; 3.1.44).

The only significant departure from the pattern of a mutually satisfying exchange of talented performance for money comes when Feste tries to deliver to Sebastian a message intended for Cesario. Feste's words, of course, make no sense at all to Sebastian, who in exasperation tips the fool in an effort to get rid of him:

> I prithee, foolish Greek, depart from me.
> There's money for thee. If you tarry longer,
> I shall give worse payment.
>
> (4.1.18)

Instead of begging for more or invoking a witty blessing on his benefactor, this time Feste responds with open contempt: "By my troth, thou hast an open hand. These wise men that give fools money get themselves a good report—after fourteen years' purchase" (21). When the young man seems to deny his identity and his relationships with people in Illyria, Feste's words, his medium of exchange, lose their value, and the exchange process breaks down: "No, I do not know you, nor I am not sent to you by my lady, to bid you come speak with her, nor your name is not Master Cesario, nor this is not my nose neither: nothing that is so is so" (5). Because Sebastian cannot receive Feste's message, his offer of money is not part of a reciprocal exchange but, from his point of view, an insulting dismissal and, from Feste's, a wise man's folly.

Sebastian's refusal to participate results, of course, from Feste's mistake, not from Sebastian's rejection of the principle of reciprocity. His scenes with Antonio stress his dual awareness that taking implies an obligation to give and that gifts of love cannot be reduced to an economic transaction. "Recompense," Shakespeare's word for the idea of reciprocity, is the subject of his first speech: "My stars shine darkly over me. The malignancy of my fate might perhaps distemper yours; therefore I shall crave of you your leave, that I may bear my evils alone. It were a bad recompense for your love, to lay any of them on you" (2.1.3). He pursues isolation because he feels unable to enter into a balanced mutual relationship. But when Antonio persists in offering help and protection, Sebastian understands that rejecting such love would be unkind, although gratitude is the only recompense he can give:

> My kind Antonio,
> I can no other answer make but thanks,
> And thanks; and ever oft good turns
> Are shuffled off with such uncurrent pay;
> But were my worth as is my conscience firm,
> You should find better dealing.
>
> (3.3.13)

Similarly, Sebastian values the pearl Olivia gives him as symbol of the wonder of her love and reciprocates by vowing eternal love.

Thus the transfer of wealth from one person to another in *Twelfth Night* creates and expresses a wide variety of relationships: entertainer with audience, employer with employee, friend with friend, and husband with wife. Concomitantly, repudiating the principle of reciprocity signals the breakdown of community and the outbreak of hostility. The extreme case is

Antonio, who is excluded from Illyria because he refuses to repay what he has taken from Duke Orsino. His offence, he explains to Sebastian,

> might have since been answer'd in repaying
> What we took from them, which for traffic's sake
> Most of our city did. Only myself stood out,
> For which if I be lapsed in this place
> I shall pay dear.
>
> (3.3.33)

Antonio knows that because he has refused to repay, he will pay dearly if he is recognized, for the ugly reverse of the reciprocity binding people harmoniously together is the requital of injury with injury in a divisive cycle of revenge. Similarly, when it appears that Sebastian is unwilling to return his purse, Antonio's love turns to hostility. The refusal is a denial of their relationship, and to claim no relationship is to create a hostile one. Antonio has sincerely believed his love to be totally selfless and his generosity to expect no return. But in the crisis produced by Orsino's revenge and by the confusion of brother and sister, he discovers that he has counted on receiving loyalty and gratitude in return for giving Sebastian "his life" and "my love" (5.1.80, 81). Without such recompense love is impossible, and his adulation is transformed to scorn.

Sir Toby's relationship with Andrew Aguecheek also demonstrates the principle of reciprocity by negative example. Toby coaxes money from the thin-faced knight, who receives nothing in return but deceptive assurances of success in his courtship of Olivia. Because Toby is exploitative and Andrew foolish, we see their companionship as a travesty of friendship, and its disintegration in the last act strikes us as no loss and no surprise. Toby's high-spirited gaiety is equalled by his selfish disregard for other people, but even he realizes that "pleasure will be paid, one time or another," and he marries Maria "in recompense" (5.1.364) for her part in the gulling of Malvolio.

Only Malvolio stands outside the lines of exchange that link the characters in increasingly complex patterns of relationship. He is the only major character who pays Feste nothing and neither gives nor receives a gift. He lacks the "generous" and "free" temperament that provides a sense of proportion, as Olivia tells him (1.5.91, 92), but he is no more greedy than Sir Toby, who calculates that he has cost Sir Andrew "some two thousand . . . or so" (3.2.54–55), or than Sir Andrew, who expects to repair his fortune by marrying Olivia. The measure of Malvolio's self-love is not his miserliness or covetousness but his presumptuous belief that he lives in a sphere above and beyond ordinary human relationships. Maria's attempts to define what is so odious about Malvolio (he is a "puritan" and a "time-pleaser" [2.3.140, 148]) at first sound contradictory, if a puritan is one who self-righteously condemns lapses from a moral ideal and a "time-pleaser" one who cynically manipulates worldly affairs for self-aggrandizement. But Maria is right both times; the puritan and the politician meet in Malvolio's self-esteem and in his contempt for people and for human relationships as ends in themselves. This total lack of identification with other people both incites and provides the means for Malvolio's gulling. When his insults provoke the conspirators to revenge, they can easily persuade him that Fortune has singled him out for greatness. Maria's letter merely reinforces his desire to "wash off gross acquaintance" and his assumption that he condescends to speak to ordinary mortals as "nightingales answer daws" (2.5.162–63; 3.4.35–36).

In *Twelfth Night* money symbolizes not love so much as a broader engagement with the real and imperfect world; paying, lending, giving, and taking are signs of willingness to have commerce with human society. Because the attitude that controls Malvolio's response to other people is "I am not of your element" (3.4.124), he does not take part in the exchanges of wealth that engage the other characters. Even when he is duped into believing that Olivia has given him her love and, by marrying him, will give him wealth and power, he feels no obligation or gratitude. He thanks "Jove" and "my stars" (2.5.172), but not Olivia. He believes that "nothing that can be can come between me and the full prospect of my hopes" (3.4.81) and that no human actions, not even his own, contribute to this perfect felicity.

The success of the plot against him teaches Malvolio the vulnerability he shares with the rest of mankind. In his distress he appeals to Feste for help, and promises, "I will live to be thankful to thee for't"; "It shall advantage thee"; "I'll requite it in the highest degree" (4.2.82, 111, 118). A demonstration of dependency so humiliating and a promise to reciprocate offered under duress do not promise Malvolio's sudden conversion to brotherly love, but even his departing curse, "I'll be reveng'd on the whole pack of you" (5.1.378), does not inspire, in the theatre, the dread or pathos critics often solemnly attribute to it. Malvolio may never learn with Prospero that "the rarer action is / In virtue than in vengeance," but even his comically impotent fury registers his dawning awareness that he is "one of their kind" (*The Tempest*, 5.1.27–28, 23). In suffering wrong and experiencing the natural human desire to hurt back, he is at least entering the rough give and take of the real world. And Olivia's immediate sympathy and

Orsino's command to "Pursue him, and entreat him to a peace" (5.1.380) assure the audience, I think, of future reconciliation.

While all the characters take part in the process of exchange, Viola is distinguished by her fuller understanding of the conscious and unconscious operation of the principle of reciprocity. Hating ingratitude more than any other vice, she repays Orsino's trust and favour with loyal service, faithfully wooing Olivia for him despite her own longing to be his wife. And the heart of her plea to Olivia is that love deserves recompense; "My master, not myself, lacks recompense" (1.5.285), she replies tartly when Olivia offers to tip her. However great Olivia's beauty, she argues, Orsino's love could be "but recompens'd" (253) by winning her. Indeed, Viola breaks through Olivia's reserve by teaching her that the gifts of nature too bring an obligation to give in return, "for what is yours to bestow is not yours to reserve" (188). The lesson Olivia learns, "ourselves we do not owe" (310), strikingly resembles the "basic theme" which Marcel Mauss's English editor finds in the anthropologist's analysis of reciprocity: "One belongs to others and not to oneself." Still, for all Viola's advocacy of the human obligation to love and to give, it is impossible for her to reciprocate the love Olivia gives to Cesario, a fiction Viola has created. And she begins to regret her male disguise when she realizes the falseness of her position in relation to Olivia. As Cesario she clearly tells Olivia that she can never love her but, even so, she accepts Olivia's gifts, sparing her the pain and humiliation of having these symbols of love rejected.

Viola, then, understands that we cannot take without giving, but she knows also that giving may not be as selfless as it appears. Just as she sincerely tries to persuade Olivia to reciprocate Duke Orsino's love, she tries to show him the arrogance of his stubborn refusal to accept rejection. When Olivia refuses to return his love, his insistence that he "cannot be so answer'd" (2.4.88) reveals his noble passion to be, at least in part, a determination to dominate and an egoist's conviction that reality must conform to his will. Although Orsino does not recognize the self-glorification in his unrequited love for Olivia, when he speaks of Olivia paying a "debt of love" (1.1.33) to her brother or when he advises Cesario against loving a woman "not worth thee" (2.4.27), he assumes that people seek a return of equivalent or greater value for the love they give. Because Viola is fully conscious that giving love involves asking for love, she denies herself the joy of offering her love to Orsino.

Recognizing the reciprocal nature of human relationships, then, does not solve all problems. It is impossible to give without desiring some return, but to expect exact recompense, as Feste demonstrates to Fabian, makes an absurd sham of giving: "to give a dog and in recompense desire my dog again" (5.1.6). Giving without recompense may be self-indulgent, insulting, foolish, or tyrannical, but failing to give is self-destructive, as Viola reminds us, describing her father's daughter who "never told her love, / But let concealment like a worm i' th' bud / Feed on her damask cheek" (2.4.110).

Not even Viola, then, can discover a way out of the tangled personal relationships that make up the plot of *Twelfth Night*. Beneficent fortune, not human wit, creates the happy ending. It is the fact that Sebastian exists, rather than moral education or spiritual growth, that solves the problems troubling the inhabitants of Illyria. The sorting out of couples in the last scene, however, is not merely a mechanically-contrived happy ending; it is, rather, the culmination of the reciprocal exchanges I have been tracing. In the course of the action, all the major characters have been tempted by the dream of self-sufficiency, but have been forced, by circumstances and by their own needs and desires, into relationships where they become aware of their obligations to and dependence on others. Viola-Cesario is the key figure in the process. She triggers Olivia's abandonment of her vows of celibacy and provides her with the humbling experience of finding the real world intractable to her will. She provides Orsino with real human love as an alternative to a self-centred fantasy. When all fantasies of limitless personal power and happiness collapse in the last scene under the pressure of the destructive aspect of reciprocity, Orsino and Olivia are ready to relinquish their dreams of Olivia and Cesario for the real love of Viola and Sebastian. Finally repelled from worshipping at "uncivil" Olivia's "ingrate . . . altars" (5.1.112, 113), Orsino's first reaction is the angry cruelty that is so often the corollary of sentimentality. But when Sebastian's arrival reveals Viola's identity, he asks for Viola's hand and gives her his in grateful recompense for "service done him" (321).

The sudden reversal from hostility and disintegrating relationships to love and alliance results from the amazing yet natural division of Cesario into Viola and Sebastian. This separation of brother and sister into two independent people symbolically illustrates Lévi-Strauss's theory that the principle of reciprocity binds people together in stable societies through the prohibition of incest and its wider social application, the custom of exogamy. He speculates that incest "in the broadest sense of the word, consists in obtaining by oneself, and for oneself, instead of by another, and for another." The functional value of reciprocal exchange in marriage alliances and of the prohibition of marriage within certain degrees is to maintain "the group as a group, . . . avoiding the indefinite fission and segmentation which the practice of consanguineous marriages would bring about."

So too in *Twelfth Night*, it is only when Olivia's exclusive allegiance to her brother is relinquished, and when brother and sister are brought together so that they can be publicly divided, that a harmonious and cohesive society becomes possible. The strangers from across the sea rescue the native Illyrians both from the sterility of self-preoccupation and from the divisive violence of their inevitable conflicts. Viola and Sebastian free Orsino and Olivia from illusions of exclusive self-fulfilment and total dominance and give them instead the shared happiness of mutual love. Neither Shakespeare nor the anthropologists claim that awareness of the principle of reciprocity can fundamentally alter the finite, complex nature of the human condition, but in his last romantic comedy Shakespeare suggests that by understanding our mutual needs we can choose love, generosity, and alliance rather than isolation, stagnation, and division.

Language, Theme, and Character in *Twelfth Night*

Elizabeth M. Yearling

With the English language's growth in power and importance in the six-teenth and seventeenth centuries came a zest for theorizing about the truth of words. Some writers continued to stress the benefits of eloquence, one of the more recent acquisitions of English. Francis Meres asserts in *Palladis Tamia* (1598) that "though the naked truth be welcome, yet it is more gratefull, if it come attired and adorned with fine figures, and choice phrases." Sixteenth-century grammar schools taught moral truth through eloquence, emphasizing authors "who at the same time polish and teach language and morals." The compatibility of words and motives are accepted in guides to conduct such as William Martyn's *Youths Instruction* (1612) which states that "the inward cogitations of a mans hart are publikely revealed by his speech, and outward actions." But Martyn's axiom can be juxtaposed with any number of versions of *Politeuphuia*'s "The typ of the tongue soundeth not alwayes the depth of the heart." And although rhet-oric, the art of eloquence, could be seen as a means for communicating the truth effectively, the new fashionable teachers of logic and rhetoric, Ramus and his school, were inclined to treat rhetoric as the art of dissimulation. "Matter" became more important than words. Bacon writes that words "are but the images of matter; and except they have life of reason and invention, to fall in love with them is all one as to fall in love with a picture." Words were more likely to be trusted if they were plain. "Pure and neat Language I love, yet plaine and customary," claimed Ben Jonson; "*An Innocent* man needs no *Eloquence*."

From *Shakespeare Survey: An Annual Survey of Shakespearean Study and Production,* volume 35, edited by Stanley Wells. © 1982 by the Estate of Elizabeth Yearling. Cambridge University Press, 1982.

While many theorists anticipated the demands of the Royal Society for words to represent things, there was also interest in the idea expounded in Plato's *Cratylus* that the names of things already possessed "natural correctness," an idea which Plato supported with various etymologies false and true. One of the most important revaluations of Spenser's language, by Martha Craig, argues that his linguistic innovations and alterations accord with Platonic theory ("The Secret Wit of Spenser's Language," in *Elizabethan Poetry*, ed. Paul J. Alpers). Here is an ideal way in which words represent things.

By the turn of the century it was acknowledged that words should not simply adorn, but should convey matter and truth. Even Lyly, the most notorious stylist of the late sixteenth century, stresses his content: "Though the style nothing delight the dainty ear of the curious sifter, yet will the matter recreate the mind of the courteous reader." It became fashionable to decry eloquence and to praise a plain, unassuming style. But theory has to be tested in practice. The greatest practitioner of the period, Shakespeare, happened to be a playwright, and drama, where the author does not directly address readers or audience, has its special problems. The dramatist needs many styles, not just one plain style. He can allow his villains to exploit deceptive words, but he must also find words for his heroes and heroines, who usually need to speak more than Cordelia's "nothing." He cannot embark on a diction which expresses the essence of things. Spenser's technique is a matter for the study, often—as with his spelling—for eye rather than ear. Shakespeare has to find ways of communicating truth which are more complex than any theoretical straightforward relationship of word and subject-matter.

His problems are aired—semi-seriously—in *Twelfth Night*. Halfway through the play, Viola and Feste meet and jest about words and meaning (3.1.1–60). The significance of their exchange is uncertain. T. W. Craik [in the Arden Shakespeare] writes that the encounter sounds like "a warming-up after a theatrical interval." Yet this is the only meeting between Shakespeare's heroine and his fool. Their quibbling shows the two-facedness of words. Feste comments on how quickly "the wrong side" of a sentence "may be turned outward." His own punning on Viola's description of words as "wanton"—"equivocal"—turns to absurdity the idea that words equal things. He worries about his sister's name since "her name's a word, and to dally with that word might make my sister wanton." He uses his theory that "words are very rascals" to avoid justifying his opinion, for "words are grown so false, I am loath to prove reason with them." The debate itself embodies the slipperiness of words, and the confusion is compounded when Feste admits to being Olivia's "corrupter of words." His trade is to use words deceptively, and what he says cannot be trusted. Shakespeare makes it difficult to take the scene seriously.

Yet often in *Twelfth Night* he shows words to be frivolous, conventional, or false. Apart from Feste's comments there is Olivia's remark about the poetical being "the more like to be feigned" (1.5.197). Occasionally characters use words as mere decoration. The most blatant example is Sir Andrew, who stores useful vocabulary such as the "odours," "pregnant," and "vouchsafed," of Viola's greeting to Olivia (3.1.92). Feste punctures words which he finds swollen. "Vent thy folly somewhere else," Sebastian snaps incautiously, and is punished by some sarcastic variations on "vent" which must cure him of the verb (4.1.10–17). Feste's mockery can conceal further jokes. To Viola he remarks, "who you are and what you would are out of my welkin. I might say 'element,' but the word is overworn" (3.1.58–60). "Welkin" too is an old-fashioned, poetic word. The overworn noun "element" is used by several characters, from Viola to Malvolio. A time bomb has been set for Malvolio's pompous "I am not of your element" (3.4.125).

But tired or inflated vocabulary brings us to one of the play's complexities. A rich source of cliché was the language of compliment, the store of polite but often insincere courtesies which came naturally to the well-bred but had to be taught to the uncourtly in manuals which suggested the right phrases for wooing and suing. And it is the heroine who is the play's main speaker in this fossilized, conventional style. Olivia rejects Viola's address:

> VIOLA. Cesario is your servant's name, fair princess.
> OLIVIA. My servant, sir? 'Twas never merry world
> Since lowly feigning was call'd compliment:
> Y'are servant to the Count Orsino, youth.

She could also have criticized the fashionable epithet, "fair." Viola justifies her use of "servant" by explaining the word literally:

> And he is yours, and his must needs be yours:
> Your servant's servant is your servant, madam.
>
> (3.1.99–104)

The sentence Viola turns into a neat excuse was still paraded as a compliment halfway through the century, in Philomusus's *The Academy of Compliments* (1646): "Sir, I am the servant of your servants." And Viola's "vouchsafed," so admired by Sir Andrew, is something of an affectation. The verb "vouchsafe" means "grant in a condescending manner" and was appropriate between subject and monarch but less fitting in other relationships. Its use is mocked as overdeferential by many Elizabethan and Jacobean dramatists. Much of Viola's language, especially to Olivia, is affected, courtly, artificial, not the style we expect of a Shakespearean heroine. But Shakespeare exploits this conventional speech brilliantly. In act 1, scene 5, Viola's speeches in praise of Olivia are full of stock poetic phrases: "red and white," "cruell'st she alive," "sighs of fire," "call upon my soul," "contemned love" (242–80). She borrows the standard phraseology of the sonnet-writers. But she also mocks herself. She worries about whether she is speaking to the right woman, and claims she is anxious to complete her penned speech. The scene turns on Viola's semi-serious use of conventional vocabulary and images, her knowledge of what she is doing, and our share in that knowledge. Yet there is more. The stereotyped language conveys a considerable depth of feeling. "'Tis beauty truly blent" is a genuine appreciation of Olivia's beauty and of Viola's task as a rival. "Make me a willow cabin" is a powerful love speech. The strength and truth of feeling make it wrong to concentrate on the clichés and stock motifs, or on the speech's deception. Viola uses words devalued by overexposure; she speaks them as Cesario, whose existence is illusory, but their emotion convinces. We must add to Olivia's remark that the poetical is "like to be feigned," Touchstone's ambiguous words in *As You Like It:* "the truest poetry is the most feigning" (3.3.16).

Viola's poetry shows us Shakespeare's success in using falsehood to communicate truth. She deceives Olivia. Yet the audience, though undeceived, receives from the same language a sense of shared and genuine emotion. There is another way in which Viola's words communicate a truth. Her style expresses her nature. She is a linguistic chameleon who adapts her style to her companion. Her vocabulary ranges from courtly compliment to rude jargon (1.5.205). But her variousness is not just verbal: her nature is to deal confidently with sudden changes. And the assumed registers, coupled often with sincere feelings, capture the blend of truth and illusion which Viola represents. It is difficult not to see a convincing personality breaking through the polite fiction which is Cesario. This is most notable in Viola's discussion of love with Orsino in act 2, scene 4, but even the play's less spectacular passages can take us below Cesario's surface. After Antonio, in the belief that she is Sebastian, has interrupted her reluctant duelling, he asks for his money:

> VIOLA. What money, sir?
> For the fair kindness you have show'd me here,

> And part being prompted by your present trouble,
> Out of my lean and low ability
> I'll lend you something. My having is not much;
> I'll make division of my present with you.
> Hold, there's half my coffer.
>
> (3.4.349–55)

The last line echoes, with an important difference, Antonio's "Hold, sir, here's my purse" (3.3.38). Antonio's was a gift of unqualified generosity to a friend. Viola's is a carefully thought-out loan to a helpful but puzzling stranger. She moves slowly towards the offer. "I'll lend" is preceded by a series of subordinate clauses and phrases outlining her reasons and stressing her poverty. "My having is not much" repeats the content of the line before, and adds to our impression that Viola feels an uncomfortable need to justify herself. Her next speech contrasts in its vehemence. Antonio reminds Viola of his former "kindnesses."

> VIOLA.   I know of none,
> Nor know I you by voice or any feature.
> I hate ingratitude more in a man
> Than lying, vainness, babbling drunkenness,
> Or any taint of vice whose strong corruption
> Inhabits our frail blood.
>
> (3.4.361–66)

There is no delay in reaching the point here. The verbs come first, several of them, forcefully stating an immediate reaction. We are persuaded that the speaker is not the illusory Cesario. No courteous surface falsifies these emotions.

Although *Twelfth Night* includes Feste's scepticism and many instances of verbal folly and deception, Shakespeare's practice encourages a positive belief in the power of words. Character and theme emerge from the nature of the words and the way they are combined. Here we are a little closer to the Platonic theory of names. Several characters in *Twelfth Night* have an individual vocabulary and syntax. Orsino's relatively short part in the play contains a high proportion of new and often slightly pompous words. In act 1, scene 4, he praises Viola's youthful appearance: "Diana's lip / Is not more smooth and *rubious*"; "And all is *semblative* a woman's part" (31–34). In act 2, scene 4, he contributes "cloyment" to the stodgy line, "That suffers surfeit, cloyment, and revolt" (100). Act 5, scene 1 brings more new vocabulary—"baubling" and "unprizable" describe Antonio's ship (52–53);

Olivia, the "marble-breasted" tyrant (122), casts his faith to "non-regardance" (119). New words are common in Orsino's vocabulary, especially words of several syllables ending in suffixes. His syntax is appropriate. Barbara Hardy notes his long sentences and sustained images, characteristics which are marked in the first scene. He uses little colloquial, easy speech.

Sir Toby is an interesting contrast. He also invents long words—"substractors" (1.3.34), "consanguineous" (2.3.78), "intercepter" (3.4.224). And his syntax is mannered. He teases Sir Andrew: "Wherefore are these things hid? Wherefore have these gifts a curtain before 'em? Are they like to take dust, like Mistress Mall's picture? Why dost thou not go to church in a galliard, and come home in a coranto?" (1.3.122–26). The rhetorical questions and repeated "wherefore" are part of a complete repetition of meaning in the first two questions, and there is syntactical balance in the last sentence. Sir Toby likes to put nouns in pairs, which sometimes alliterate: "they are scoundrels and substractors" (1.3.34); "he's a coward and a coistrel" (1.3.40). But Sir Toby's long words and patterned syntax are not enough to elevate his speech. His long words occur in prose, not verse, and their use undercuts their impressiveness: "substractor" is a nonce-word meaning "detractor" and it *sounds* like a drunken fumbling for words. Another good word to tumble over is "consanguineous" which is accompanied by a gentle parody of the scholar's habit of pairing foreign imports with simpler words: "Am not I consanguineous? Am I not of her blood?" M. M. Mahood notes [in the Penguin edition] that "exquisite" (2.3.142) is "a difficult word for the drunken knights to get their tongues round." The same must be true of Sir Toby's compliment to Maria: "Good night, Penthesilea" (2.3.177). The polysyllables are undermined by being spoken drunkenly, and also by the company they keep, since Sir Toby's speeches contain popular phrases and words of low origin. He is recorded as the first literary user of "bum-baily" (3.4.178), the meanest kind of bailiff, a title which must have been current in the least reputable areas of London. His first words are "What a plague" (1.3.1); he tells Malvolio to "Sneck up!" (2.3.94); he uses the vulgar phrase "call me cut" (2.3.187), and colloquial words such as "coistrel" (1.3.40). He is also the play's most frequent user of the second person pronoun "thou" instead of the more formal "you."

Sir Toby's speech mixes impressive vocabulary and mannered syntax with colloquial words. It reflects his disorder but at the same time a certain openness to experience. Malvolio's language indicates constraint. He introduces fewer new words than either Orsino or Sir Toby, but his mouth is full of pompous phrases and long words without the poetry of Orsino or the colloquialism of Sir Toby. He is at his worst in contemplation, in the letter scene (2.5.23–179). Inflated vocabulary is not simply a public front but is his very nature. "A look round" becomes "a demure travel of regard," "what do these letters mean?" becomes "what should that alphabetical position portend?" Long abstract words abound: "there is no consonancy in the sequel; that suffers under probation." The homelier words of his tirade in act 2, scene 3 are there only to signify his disgust: "Have you no wit, manners, nor honesty, but to gabble like tinkers at this time of night? Do ye make an ale-house of my lady's house, that ye squeak out your coziers' catches without any mitigation or remorse of voice?" (88–92). His style is noun-laden: nouns come in strings or separated by the preposition "of." The change when he woos Olivia (3.4.17–55) is interesting. He is still pompous and noun-obsessed—"this does make some obstruction in the blood"—but he throws in the fashionable word "sweet" and quotes fragments of popular songs: "Please one, and please all," "Ay, sweetheart, and I'll come to thee." Here he uses the familiar "thou," unthinkable from a servant to his lady. The visible changes in appearance and behaviour are accompanied by more subtle changes in his language.

Other characters have personal styles. Sir Andrew, magpie-like, purloins impressive words, misuses long words (5.1.179–80), and tends to echo the speaker before him (1.3.62–63, 2.3.56). Feste parodies his superiors' polysyllables: "I did impeticos thy gratillity" (2.3.27). He demands Olivia's attention to Malvolio's letter with the words "perpend, my princess" (5.1.298), mocking—M. P. Tilley argues—the style of Cambyses. And he produces nonsense names, "Pigrogromitus" (2.3.23), "Quinapalus" (1.5.33). His verbal whimsy complicates the debate about words. His attacks on words and their falsehood tell us more about Feste than about words.

When we read or hear Twelfth Night we learn about the characters by attending to their vocabulary and syntax. Besides expressing character, the words and sentence structure can also clarify themes. One of the play's contrasts is between holiday and the work-a-day world. Although the title suggests festivity, recent criticism has qualified C. L. Barber's treatment of Twelfth Night as a festive comedy. Many modern critics dwell on the play's melancholy mood, but in more positive opposition to festivity are the characters' working lives. Sir Toby and Sir Andrew hope that life "consists of eating and drinking" (2.3.11–12), but their fellows have more to do. Even Orsino, who has let his dukedom rule itself, at last resumes his function as ruler and magistrate. Viola is kept hard at work, Feste too—and when he is absent without leave he is threatened with dismissal. Malvolio and Maria have duties in Olivia's household, and Olivia has that household to organize (4.3.16–20).

The contrast between holiday and work results in an interesting structural device. There are repeated movements from musing or conversation back to some necessary task. These shifts are embodied in the dialogue, and centre on Viola. It is easy to note the difference between the first scene's languor and the second scene's sense of purpose, but even within scene 2 there is a distinct change of mood. Viola and the Captain discuss her brother's fate and she is encouraged to hope for his safety:

> Mine own escape unfoldeth to my hope,
> Whereto thy speech serves for authority,
> The like of him.
>
> (1.2.19–21)

The lines are in verse, the first has a formal old-fashioned -*eth* verb ending, and the object is delayed by a subordinate clause. Viola then switches to practical questions about her present situation: "Know'st thou this country?"; "Who governs here?" The crisper -*s* ending for the third-person verb belongs with the simple questions and short prose lines which contrast with the Captain's verse replies. Viola's interest in what has or may have happened to her brother is superseded by a need to sort out her own affairs, and her style changes correspondingly. She installs herself in Orsino's service. As his attendant she has opportunities for leisurely talk, but she keeps remembering there are things to be done. In act 1, scene 5, she is Orsino's messenger to Olivia. At first she fences with Olivia but she suddenly returns to duty:

> OLIVIA. Are you a comedian?
> VIOLA. No, my profound heart: and yet, by the very fangs of
>   malice I swear, I am not that I play. Are you the lady of
>   the house?

Her ambiguity about herself is accompanied by an obscure oath. With her question, the conversation becomes more straightforward, only to dissolve in wordplay again.

> OLIVIA. If I do not usurp myself, I am.
> VIOLA. Most certain, if you are she, you do usurp yourself: for
>   what is yours to bestow is not yours to reserve.

Viola's quibble is followed by an explanation both antithetical and cryptic. But then she changes to short statement—"But this is from my commission"—and a plain declaration of intent: "I will on with my speech in your praise, and then show you the heart of my message" (1.5.183–92). Similarly her debate with Feste is interrupted by the direct question, "Is thy lady within?" Here too the preceding sentence is syntactically more elaborate and plays on words. Feste prays that Jove might send Cesario a beard and Viola replies: "By my troth, I'll tell thee, I am almost sick for one, [*Aside*] though I would not have it grow on my chin" (3.1.45–49). In act 2, scene 4, the discussion of love with Orsino, and the story of Cesario's "sister," draw to a close with Viola's

> I am all the daughters of my father's house,
> And all the brothers too: and yet I know not.

The riddle is couched in repeated phrase-patterns—"all the daughters," "all the brothers"—followed by a virtual aside. After this we are bound to read a meditative pause till Viola sharply changes the subject: "Sir, shall I to this lady?" (2.4.121–23). On each of these occasions brief statements and questions replace more complex syntax, often punning or patterned. Viola delights in conversation and jesting debate but is aware of her present duty.

Other characters move similarly into action. Olivia's style in act 1, scene 5, also involves syntactical contrasts although her questions are misleadingly direct. She lingers over jokes such as the inventory of her beauty, but follows with a pertinent question: "Were you sent hither to praise me?" (1.5.252–53). She continues with what seem to be the same sort of inquiries: "How does he love me?"; "Why, what would you?"; "What is your parentage?" (258, 271, 281). She is pursuing what has become important to her, but she has moved from the interview's business—Orsino—to Cesario-Viola, and she stops herself with crisp commands and statements which are more to the immediate purpose.

> Get you to your lord:
> I cannot love him: let him send no more,
> Unless, perchance, you come to me again,
> To tell me how he takes it. Fare you well:
> I thank you for your pains: spend this for me.
> (1.5.283–87)

The short clauses emphasize her businesslike manner. The syntax is more flowing only in the lines where she provides for a return by Cesario, who distracts her from the task of rejecting Orsino, and she couches these lines in the conditional. The lingering "unless" added to the brusque "let him send no more" captures her feelings. During her second meeting with Viola, Olivia's ears recall her from distracting thoughts.

> O world, how apt the poor are to be proud!
> If one should be a prey, how much the better
> To fall before the lion than the wolf! [*Clock strikes.*]
> The clock upbraids me with the waste of time.
> Be not afraid, good youth, I will not have you,
> And yet when wit and youth is come to harvest,
> Your wife is like to reap a proper man.
> There lies your way, due west.
>
> (3.1.129–36)

Again complex writing—subordination, apostrophe, extended metaphor—accompanies the musing. Simple statements interrupt it. We may compare with Olivia's "waste of time" the First Officer's short, impatient sentences when his prisoner Antonio procrastinates: "What's that to us? The time goes by. Away!" (3.4.373). These people do not have all the time in the world. Tasks and duties press on them. Even Sebastian, who has nothing in particular to do in Illyria, is not prepared just to stand talking to Antonio. Again the transition is sudden; again questions replace conditionals and balanced phrases.

> But were my worth, as is my conscience, firm,
> You should find better dealing. What's to do?
> Shall we go see the relics of this town?
>
> (3.3.17–19)

Note especially "What's to *do*?" He is later caught up in Olivia's urge to action when she decides to marry him. His meditative speech, "This is the air, that is the glorious sun" (4.3.1 ff.), is cut off by her arrival with a request formed like a command: "Blame not this haste of mine" (4.3.22).

Orsino's resumption of office is the most elaborate change in the speed of action. At last he comes to woo Olivia himself. But before he can talk to her he is brought some work. The officers enter with Antonio, and Orsino's questioning of that "notable pirate" is interrupted by Olivia's arrival. For the audience this is their first meeting. The Duke's reaction is oddly mechanical:

> Here comes the Countess: now heaven walks on earth.
> But for thee, fellow—fellow, thy words are madness.
>
> (5.1.95–96)

Orsino's "but" sets the matter in hand against his response to Olivia. Compare these words with the equivalent passage in William Burnaby's eighteenth-century revision of the play. There the Duke has more to say about the woman he loves:

> Now Heav'n walks on Earth, and Beauty round
> Invades us all! Each glance devotes a Slave,
> And every step, she treads upon a heart,
> All of the Skies, but pitty you have brought.
> (*Love Betray'd; or, the Agreable Disapointment*)

Burnaby's addition is heavy-handed but shows he was aware that Orsino's brief welcome in the original is a little strange. It could be argued that since Orsino seems more interested in his own moods than in Olivia, he can offer only a commonplace compliment when he actually meets her, and then directs his attention to the Antonio–Cesario conflict which fascinates him. But this is not what happens. Olivia is Orsino's business. When she appears he is needed as a magistrate and after acknowledging her briskly he returns to his case. Then, just as briskly, he quashes Antonio's complaint and reserves judgement, so that he can attend to his main concern:

> But for thee, fellow—fellow, thy words are madness.
> Three months this youth hath tended upon me;
> But more of that anon. Take him aside.
>
> (5.1.96–98)

Again simple, brusque statements announce Orsino's despatching of business, and another "but" emphasizes the transitions and oppositions of the passage. Soon, Orsino resumes his polysyllables and complex sentences.

The words and syntax of *Twelfth Night* are interesting for what they say and for what they are. The nature of the characters' vocabulary tells us something about them; the sentence structure also exposes the characters and their moods, and points at thematic oppositions. Even if their surface meaning is deceptive, words can still communicate truthfully. Yet we are also told that words deceive. And here we might note a recurring syntactic pattern which embodies the deceptions of *Twelfth Night*. Earlier I quoted "I am not that I play" from Viola's first encounter with Olivia. This takes up her request to the Captain, "Conceal me what I am" (1.2.53) and prefigures a cryptic exchange with Olivia in act 3, scene 1:

> OLIVIA. I prithee tell me what thou think'st of me.
> VIOLA. That you do think you are not what you are.

> OLIVIA. If I think so, I think the same of you.
> VIOLA. Then think you right; I am not what I am.
>
> (140–43)

The setting of negative against positive in conjunction with the verb "to be" is repeated at the end of the play when Orsino finds Sebastian and Viola forming "A natural perspective, that is, and is not!" (5.1.215). And it is mocked in Feste's joking: " 'That that is, is': so I, being Master Parson, am Master Parson; for what is 'that' but 'that'? and 'is' but 'is'?" (4.2.15–17). In fact here, that that is, is not. Feste is more accurate, but without knowing it, when he tells Sebastian, whom he mistakes for Cesario, "Nothing that is so, is so" (4.1.8–9). The repeated formula captures the confusion of actuality and fiction which these characters experience. Again the syntax tells us a truth while agreeing that words and events themselves can lie.

We cannot be certain about reality and falsehood when the genuine emotion of "My father had a daughter loved a man" can move us so. Shakespeare's achievement with language in *Twelfth Night* is to encapsulate the conflict of truth and illusion, and to remind us that facts and truth are not necessarily the same, that the truest poetry often *is* the most feigning.

The Orchestration of *Twelfth Night:* The Rhythm of Restraint and Release

Jean E. Howard

What [a consideration of thematic and psychological patterns in a play] does, and it is a useful and necessary operation, is to spatialize a temporal phenomenon, to see it in one glance as a simultaneous whole. But in experiencing a play in the theater, the audience does not start here, with a summation of the play's overriding symbolic or psychological concerns, not even if we already know the play or know other romantic comedies of its type. In the theater we begin, not with abstract reflections on the sterility of egocentricity, but with the sound of a particular kind of music and a particular man's reaction to that music. What we subsequently experience is not a psychological treatise, but a particular succession of sights, sounds, and events that create a unique theatrical experience with its own tempo, rhythm, and pauses, its own moments of engagement and detachment, and its own natural points of emphasis.

What is remarkable about this and other Shakespeare plays is the extent to which the temporal experience of them—what the play *does* in its progressive mode—constitutes and controls what the play *means.* Retrospective and progressive modes of knowing a play are not mutually exclusive. The former has about it a satisfying finality and comprehensiveness, the latter always a dynamic tentativeness; but the former rests upon the latter and should be a more integral part of theater criticism than is usually the case. What I want to do now is to examine Shakespeare's orchestration of the implied temporal enactment of *Twelfth Night* to show how a satisfying and

From *Shakespeare's Art of Orchestration: Stage Technique and Audience Response.* © 1984 by the Board of Trustees of the University of Illinois. University of Illinois Press, 1984.

meaningful theater event takes shape for the beholder. In particular, I wish to highlight how the dramaturgy of the play repeatedly whets and frustrates the theatrical appetites of the viewer so that the sense of entrapment and stasis that overtakes so many of the play's characters becomes part of the audience's own theatrical experience and is used to focus attention on the *causes* of inaction both within the world of the play and within the theater event.

As I have already noted, *Twelfth Night* begins with music. It also concludes with a song and is informed by music throughout: Toby's catches, Feste's songs for Orsino, Sir Topas's gleeful songs for the imprisoned Malvolio. Music becomes a recurrent element in the play's unfolding—a means of creating particular local effects—but also a device for providing continuity or contrast between stage moments that may otherwise be widely separated. It thus provides a way within the forward movement of the action for inviting momentary retrospection.

When the play begins, however, the audience knows nothing of the later songs: its whole concentration is focused upon Orsino and the strains he commands to sound, to stop, to sound again, and once more to cease. There could not be a more economical way of crystalizing for the audience the mood in Orsino's court or the outlines of his temperament. He is an aesthete, too overwhelmed by the emotional power of a single "dying fall" either to endure the piece's completion or even to find refreshment in the repetition of what he has just heard. The audience cannot lose itself in the music. It sounds too briefly and with too many interruptions from Orsino. In fact, we are probably impatient that he fails to allow the piece to end.

Quite clearly, it is not the music itself but Orsino's response to it to which the playwright is directing our attention. Music for the count is unmistakably a vehicle for emotional self-indulgence. He surfeits with sounds, and when they cease, he turns to language for a release of pent-up emotion. But when he talks, what becomes immediately apparent, again, is the preciosity of his sensibility. Music is food to be consumed in excess; sound, synesthetically, is like the wind carrying the smell of violets; love is like the capacious sea; he himself is like a hart pursued by the hounds of love. Metaphor and simile pile on top of one another, and Valentine's description of Olivia attempting to pickle her brother's memory in the brine of salt tears is but the capstone of the scene's metaphorical absurdities. It is with some relief that the audience leaves Orsino heading off to lie in a bed of flowers at the scene's end. More than forty-two lines of such heady stuff and the audience would probably recoil in disgust.

When Shakespeare so chooses, he can be wonderfully economical in creating striking openings for his plays. In *Twelfth Night* it is not gripping plot developments but an arresting stage mood that initially commands attention. Orsino's Illyria is an emotional hothouse. Music and language are used to reveal an overwrought, self-indulgent psyche and a court devoted solely to the care and feeding of its count's emotional excesses. There is much here to interest an audience, but not much to engage its sympathies deeply. The brevity of the scene, the artificiality of its rhetoric, even the breaking off of its music are all devices for keeping an audience at some distance from what it is watching and hearing, even as the stasis and enervation of this court are indelibly impressed upon us.

What Shakespeare then does is present two scenes in which, again, relatively little happens. They are not linked together narratively, but they afford further tonal contrasts with the play's opening segment. The orchestration of the play's first three scenes, in fact, depends heavily upon the principle of contrast for its effectiveness. Successively the audience sees three groups of characters in three locales: Orsino and his followers in his court, Viola and the seamen on the coast, Toby and his friends at Olivia's house. Each succeeding scene is longer than the last (42 lines, 64 lines, 127 lines); and each is pitched in a different key, that is, each uses language in a strikingly different way to produce distinct tonal and kinetic effects. The differences are felt primarily because of the context the first segment establishes for the audience's perception of the next two. As Mark Rose has noted, if you reverse scenes 1 and 2, which was done in at least one production he had seen, Viola's conversation with the sailors loses much of its theatrical effectiveness. It becomes functionally one-dimensional. It serves to set up the Viola plot, but it no longer provides a refreshing shift of pace and mood from what precedes it.

Viola, in her genuinely distressful situation, wastes little time in self-pity or self-display. She reaches out to know and establish a place for herself in her alien environment. Many of her speeches are questions: "What country, friends, is this?" (1.2.1); "And what should I do in Illyria?" (3); "What think you, sailors?" (5); "Know'st thou this country?" (21); "Who governs here?" (24); "What is his name?" (26); "What's she?" (35). Her situation known as thoroughly as it can be, Viola decides on a course of action: "I'll serve this Duke" (55). The future, of course, is not all known. She says: "What else may hap, to time I will commit" (60). But she has done her best to place herself in a position of readiness: though the manly garb she will assume will confine her in unforeseen ways, it also cloaks her vulnerability.

The energy and stringency of the scene are primarily conveyed by the language employed as that language is heard against the aural ground provided by Orsino's lovesick mooning. The rhetoric of scene 2 contains no conceits and hardly any metaphors, and it is swiftly propelled forward by Viola's logical questions. Language here is used as a means of finding out information and making decisions, not as a means of flaunting one's emotional sensitivity. After Orsino's speeches, it serves to heighten the audience's opinion of Viola. Vulnerable she may be, but she is not mired in an emotional bog.

When Toby, Maria, and then Andrew next come into view, the texture of what the audience hears undergoes another marked change. This is a scene of banter; in 1.3 language is used for play, and the poetry of the two preceding scenes gives way to prose. The longest speech in this segment is Toby's nine line exhortation to Andrew to demonstrate his talents in dancing; and for the most part the scene is devoted to quick-flying jests, though Maria's and Toby's fly somewhat faster, to be sure, than do Andrew's. Against the aural ground established by the businesslike dispatch of Viola's first appearance, the lighthearted expansiveness of this below-stairs world stands out sharply. Here, care is peremptorily banished as an enemy to life; and if a fat man is cast as Toby, as often occurs, his considerable girth becomes, like Falstaff's, a visual emblem of a life lived outside "the modest limits of order" (7–8). The scene itself sprawls; it is two or three times the length of the two that precede it, and what inner tension it has derives from wordplay and the exercise of nimble wits turning randomly to whatever topic lays to hand, not from Viola's purposeful march of questions.

What Shakespeare has done by stringing these three scenes together to form the opening movement of the play is to focus audience attention, not upon plot, but upon tonal and kinetic contrasts that illuminate some of the differing attitudes toward life and some of the different ways in which energy is expended in Illyria. Certainly the three scenes set the plot going and reveal much about the temperaments of Orsino, Viola, and Toby, respectively, just as they function to set off Viola as a norm between extremes; but they also suggest, through successive aural and kinetic shifts, the tonal and kinetic parameters of this fictive world: the attitudes and impulses that are repeatedly to be played off against one another. Stultifying self-indulgence, brisk assertiveness, playful and unfettered high spirits— these are some of the dominant moods of *Twelfth Night* lightly delineated for the audience as the play begins and then set up for more complex elaboration later.

In this regard, the opening movement of *Twelfth Night* is orchestrated somewhat like the opening of *Hamlet* in which the dissimilar "worlds" of battlements, court, and Polonius's family are successively juxtaposed before the partial closure effected by a return to the battlements. In both plays the initial scenes are crafted to help the audience hear, see, and feel important differences among discrete stage groups and to recognize the tension these differences can create. Of course, the opening movements of *Hamlet* and *Twelfth Night* are not identical. The aural, visual, and kinetic disjunctions between scenes are more pronounced and unsettling in the tragedy, the emotional stakes higher; nonetheless, Shakespeare's methods of orchestration and his theatrical strategies are similar. Economically delineating differences, his stagecraft also creates a field of tension resulting not from any one scene, but from the successive juxtaposition of several. In *Hamlet* the protagonist at once feels and expresses the tension between his view of the world and that of Claudius. In *Twelfth Night* the direct articulation of tension comes later (recall, for example, the quandary of Viola in 1.5, trapped between a desire to speak freely and openly and a desire to obey her lord and mouth his tired rhetoric); but in *Twelfth Night* the audience anticipates this tension during the play's first movement. If the three initial scenes heighten, by their centrality, the poise and purposefulness of Viola, they also hint at the vulnerability of such poise by foiling it against less balanced but equally powerful modes of expression and self-assertion.

The second theatrical movement of *Twelfth Night* stretches from 1.4, Viola's first appearance in Orsino's court, to 2.5, Malvolio's discovery and reading of Maria's letter; and it is orchestrated quite differently from the opening movement. What primarily unifies this movement theatrically is an increasingly insistent dialectic, felt in the language and pacing of successive segments, between languor and action, constraint and release. Of course, on the level of plot, more "happens" in this segment than in the first three scenes, so there is a quickening of audience desire to see what will next take place. For example, Viola, disguised as Orsino's page, attracts the amorous passion of Olivia and is attracted to Orsino; Sebastian emerges unscathed from the sea and sets out for Orsino's court; and Malvolio offends both Feste and Toby in ways that cry out for retribution. Clearly, with Viola, the audience now begins to look ahead with some impatience to see how time and the dramatist will untangle these knots. Simultaneously, however, the audience lives in the "now" of a carefully orchestrated succession of stage events, and the rhythm of the second movement of the play creates a second kind of tension, largely unrelated to tension generated by the quickening narrative, through the repeated frustration of theatrical energies of both a linguistic and kinetic type.

Let me explain using some specifics. In 1.4 Viola appears in disguise. This is a crucial visual event, and good actresses usually are at pains to make it clear that a man's attire and a man's assertiveness are not entirely natural to Viola. The disguise, moreover, functions as the audience's first visual signal that Viola has done what she earlier promised she would do and that now a new phase of the action—Viola playing boy—is to begin. Further, the scene brings together what formerly had been separate: the melancholy count and the shipwrecked maiden. Most important, it becomes immediately apparent that the count and her costume inhibit the previously forthright heroine. As Orsino's page, Viola is not freely herself. Her refreshing energy is tamped down. She becomes entangled, willy-nilly, in the emotional enervation and the psychological self-indulgence of Orsino's court. In 1.4 she can neither deny Orsino's request that she woo Olivia, which she is loath to do, nor declare her own love, which she is all too eager to make plain. Orsino continues to churn out his lovesick rhetoric, but he *does* nothing in his own person to woo his lady. Instead, Viola becomes his unwilling go-between. Her exit must be an unhappy one, since now her true emotions can find no expression, and her energies must be directed to a task that gives her pain.

Act 1, scene 5, again highlights for the audience the pernicious consequences of disguise and false postures. Olivia's house is always an emotionally freer place than the count's palace; but in 1.5 the high spirits are more restrained, certainly, than when we first saw Toby rollicking with Sir Andrew and Maria. Feste is in momentary disgrace, Olivia is in mourning, and Malvolio is censorious. By wittily proving Olivia to be a fool, Feste temporarily holds in check the gravity hovering over the household, and he also wins Malvolio a reproof. But Feste cannot remove the real cloud hanging over the house: his lady's self-indulgent love of her mourner's role. When Feste proves her a fool, she bears him no ill will, but she also does not heed the real import of his words. Before Viola is admitted, Olivia calls for her veil, and her old posture is resumed. Only with Viola's entry does Olivia's true liberation from that posture become possible, and the heart of the scene is the encounter between veiled lady and disguised messenger that I briefly discussed [elsewhere].

The orchestration of this encounter makes the audience feel with great immediacy the constraining consequences of affected, false, or unnatural postures. False and evasive rhetoric permeates the scene and repeatedly stymies true communication. The result, for the theater audience, is a sense of pent-up and thwarted energies. At first, the constraints of Viola's disguise and her assigned role force her to adopt a cloying speech and a stance that she quite obviously—from her own interruptions of the script—does not find congenial. In turn, her clichéd text of love invites Olivia to sink into the sterile posture of the proud lady cynically repelling a tedious and unwanted assault. When Viola finally drops the script to tell how she would woo were she Orsino, the audience hears a marked aural shift. Viola's language surges with life, and Olivia's pose crumbles. She is released into love; and in the last thirty lines of the scene, her former hauteur gone, she asks questions and speaks with new energy and purpose.

But the audience is denied a love duet. The barrier of disguise still stands between Olivia and Cesario and makes them speak at cross purposes. Olivia begins the ancient catechism of love: "What is your parentage?" (1.5.263); Viola answers with a riddle and a lie: "Above my fortunes, yet my state is well. / I am a gentleman" (264–65). Olivia offers the beloved money, Viola rejects it with horrified disdain: "keep your purse" (270). Olivia's released emotional energy is misdirected and finds no reciprocity. At the scene's end, Viola is still trapped in her disguise; Olivia has shed one false pose only to embrace another: no more a nun, she now loves a woman whom she mistakes for a man. The audience once more *sees*—in Olivia's outstretched hand and Viola's recoil from the purse—and *hears*—in Olivia's questions and Viola's evasions—the pernicious consequences of disguise and false postures. Action is stymied; free and uncorrupted discourse is impossible; and it is the aural and visual orchestration of the encounter that directs the audience's attention to this impasse.

This long scene is followed by two short ones: the first appearance of Antonio and Sebastian, and the brief encounter in which Malvolio gives Viola the ring Olivia has sent. As with most scenes involving Sebastian and Antonio, 2.1 comes like a breath of fresh air. Throughout the play, Antonio and Sebastian assume the straightforward attitudes characteristic of Viola in her unguarded or undisguised state. In a play in which disguises, actual or psychological, proliferate, these two go undisguised, though Antonio is the figure who could logically most profit from a false front when in Orsino's country. But his function is to embody honest and selfless service. He has neither time for affected postures of the sort that afflict Malvolio, nor a nature easy with disguise of any sort. Here, as elsewhere when he and the young Sebastian appear, they speak without either artifice or excessive wit. Theirs is the discourse of plaindealing and truth, in which language reveals intention and culminates in action. Great, therefore, is the contrast between Antonio's final selfless declaration in 2.1 that he will court danger to follow Sebastian to Orsino's court, and Malvolio's peevish and selfish complaint at the beginning of 2.2 that Viola "might have saved me my pains, to have taken it [the ring] away yourself" (5–6). As many have noted, Malvolio is too self-absorbed to realize he is conveying a love token and too self-important to do his messenger's task with grace.

At the same time, the two adjoining short scenes underscore the contrasting plights of the twins. Sebastian in 2.1 casts off a false name and embraces a course of action; in 2.2 his sister receives a ring that binds her more tightly in a net of duplicity and leaves her with few options but that of passive resignation. Her soliloquy in 2.2, one of the few in the play, begins with logical inquiry, "What means this lady?" (16), and ends in a tangle leading to an impasse:

> My master loves her dearly;
> And I (poor monster) fond as much on him;
> And she (mistaken) seems to dote on me.
> What will become of this? As I am man,
> My state is desperate for my master's love.
> As I am woman (now alas the day!),
> What thriftless sighs shall poor Olivia breathe?
> O Time, thou must untangle this, not I;
> It is too hard a knot for me t'untie.
>
> (2.2.32–40)

This is an agile soliloquy, still laced with questions, as were Viola's first speeches, but now the questions cannot be answered in ways that make a course of action easy. She is stymied, left with the antitheses and paradoxes of her androgynous state. Once again, stasis has replaced movement; Sebastian and Antonio's purposeful acts are overshadowed by Viola's perplexed questions and her shrug of resignation. Where is this trapped energy to go? While the audience, knowing Sebastian lives, does not fully share Viola's feelings of entrapment, her soliloquy creates a sense of stasis and complication that sets in high relief the wild outpouring of uncomplicated high spirits which follows.

The dialectic between release and restraint that the whole second movement of the play embodies finds its final expression in the last three scenes of act 2: the midnight revels of Toby, the lovesick mooning of Orsino, and the boxtree scene. The orchestration of 2.3 and 2.4 is controlled by the various music that informs each. In 2.3, the below-stairs revelers jest, drink, and sing, in Malvolio's words, most uncivilly. They "squeak out" their "coziers' catches without any mitigation or remorse of voice" (83–84). Mitigation, in fact, is what the scene most wonderfully lacks. These are people in the mood for some excellent fooling, and so is the audience after observing Viola's becalmed and complicated situation. Sanctimonious Malvolio highlights, without really threatening, the exuberance of the revelers. They raid the wine cellar and sing carpe diem songs; he prates of manners and threatens to tattle to the lady of the house. When the scene ends with their plan to fool him with a false love letter, the audience is completely on their side and looks ahead with relish to the steward's mortification. But we are denied the immediate gratification of the plot's fulfillment, since the next scene plunks us down once again in the never changing, claustrophobic court of Orsino.

The Orsino scenes make clear that Shakespeare is effectively using both contrast and recurrence in the orchestration of this play. For the audience, the immediate impact of 2.4 is felt in terms of its contrasts with 2.3. We move from a world of prose to a world of poetry, from jests to seriousness, from light airs to a melancholy dirge, from exuberance to an energy level so throttled down that utter immobilization threatens to set in. We are back in an emotional bog, and the impression of stasis is emphasized by the freewheeling energies of the preceding scene and by the fact that the audience's expectation of the letter plot is cut off by the return to Orsino in his love melancholy. The tonal contrast between the two scenes is immense, highlighted by contrasts in music and language.

The sense we get of blocked or frustrated energy is further heightened by the fact that 2.4 deliberately uses aural cues to send the audience's mind back to the beginning of the play. There Orsino entered with the line "If music be the food of love, play on" (1.1.1); here he enters saying, "Give me some music" (2.4.1). In both cases he then goes on in highly complicated metaphors to expand upon his suffering and the immensity of his passion. The mood, the actions, the self-indulgent egotism are all unchanged, though here the clown's mocking invocation of the "melancholy god" and Viola's defense of women offer mild rebukes to Orsino's egocentric vision. Nonetheless, by recalling the beginning of the play, this scene heightens the audience's sense that in one central portion of the play's world nothing changes; no sunlight filters in; no veils are removed. If anything, the strong centripetal pull of Orsino's self-absorption seems to draw others into its orbit, and it is here that Viola tells her poignant tale of the "sister" who sat immobile and "pined in thought" (2.4.3). Viola never becomes that immobile other self, for she ends the scene setting off once more to Olivia, but she comes dangerously close here to embracing the passivity that so engulfs Orsino.

This is the longest of the scenes involving Orsino up to this point. The others, 1.1 and 1.4, are each about 40 lines; 2.4 is about 125 lines. It builds on those earlier scenes to give the audience its fullest sense of Orsino's monstrous self-love and self-indulgence. He does not hear the clown's mockery; he does not hear Viola's pain and her barely veiled declarations of love. All he hears is his own voice extolling the strength of his love, which is "as hungry as the sea / And can digest as much" (99–100). From this point in the play Orsino disappears until act 5; the play's exorcism of debilitating self-love focuses now on Malvolio, who in a sense undergoes *for* Orsino the humiliation that the count's self-absorption invites and that Olivia experiences in her own way in her misguided love for a woman. But before we leave Orsino, Shakespeare takes pains to develop fully his foolish self-absorption, while at the same time furthering the underlying theatrical dialectic of the play's second movement: its basic opposition of action and inaction, free speech and fettered speech, energy released and energy contained. When, in the specific theatrical context established by 2.3 and the preceding scene, the audience is thrust once more into this world, frustration and uneasiness build up. We wait for release, and that need is partly satisfied and partly frustrated by 2.5, the scene with Malvolio's reading of the letter that culminates the second movement of the play.

The orchestration of the boxtree scene was extensively analyzed in chapter 3 [of *Shakespeare's Art of Orchestration*]. My purpose here is, not to reexamine its basic contrapuntal structure, but to look at its place in the progressive orchestration of the whole play. Scene 5 of act 2 culminates the second movement of the play by compressing its basic dialectic into a single scene of great humor and great tension. Up to this point the audience has been experiencing, in successive scenes, a basic rhythm of restraint and release, has been hearing successive contrasts between affected and free-wheeling speech. Through the contrapuntal orchestration of 2.5 we simultaneously hear the constipated pomposity of Malvolio, imagining himself a count and unintentionally parodying the high-flown rhetoric of the real count, Orsino, and the scabrous jests and unrestrained oaths of Toby and his companions. The scene thus aurally highlights a central opposition in the play by exaggerating the affectations of the steward and the coarse energy of the observers.

As Malvolio preens, the audience takes satisfaction with the conspirators in seeing self-love so grotesquely display itself. At the same time, a certain amount of energy simply remains unreleased because the conspirators cannot leap out and laugh Malvolio into the ground without ruining their own joke. They are reduced to sputtering in the bushes, and some of the audience's laughter is directed at them in their fuming impotence. The scene helps to impart a sense of closure to this movement of the play through the terminal heightening afforded by its economical compression of warring impulses held in such effective counterpoint. But it also points attention ahead, not only to the completion of the letter trick, but to the final fulfilling eruption of pent-up energy in the public and direct unmasking of affectation and self-love.

The first two movements of *Twelfth Night*, in which Barber is quite right to note that not much happens in the way of overt action, nonetheless create a complex theatrical experience through their careful juxtaposition of different moods, verbal styles, and kinetic impulses. Through the contrastive orchestration of speech, the audience *hears* the central tension of the play between affectation and honest speech and *feels* the quick movement of wit, inquiry, and plain dealing repeatedly tamped down by an antithetical languor and self-absorption. Thematically, of course, Shakespeare is developing the opposition between egotism and selflessness, claustrophobic self absorption and self-forgetful action, as those trapped in literal disguises or unnatural poses are juxtaposed to the reckless Tobys and, less radically, to the plain-dealing Sebastians and Antonios of Illyria. But an audience first apprehends these thematic oppositions, not as neatly labeled abstractions, but as differences felt and heard in the contrastive rhythms and speech patterns of the theatrical continuum.

In effect, in the play's second movement, Shakespeare orchestrates the basic sensory components of performance to help the audience discriminate very precisely among the various characters and the attitudes toward experience they exemplify and, perhaps as important, to involve the audience experientially in the mounting frustration that eventuates in the plot from disguises and narcissism, and in the theater event from the repeated subversion of purposeful speech and the blocking of kinetic energy. In coming to the theater, audiences have a variety of appetites that crave satisfaction. Just as when we read a novel, we may want from our drama density of theme and complexity of characterization; but drama is a three-dimensional art form that also whets our sensory appetites for spectacle, for movement, for happenings of a very tangible sort. We want not only the plot but also what we see and hear to have both complexity and momentum. In *Twelfth Night*, certain of our theatrical appetites are repeatedly thwarted but, I would argue, to good purpose. The stop and start orchestration of the play's second movement—in which free speech becomes fettered, action frustrated—creates impatience that focuses attention on the sources of that frustration, especially the affectation and deceit which trammel up honest speech and forthright action. This frustration also begins to bring to the level of consciousness the very issue of what I have called the audience's theatrical appetites and makes us regard them critically.

In fact, the third movement of the play—acts 3 and 4—seems designed in part to engender in the audience various kinds of self-consciousness about its desires and stance as theatergoers. The third movement of the play contains more action and consequently is orchestrated somewhat differently than what has gone before. The movement begins slowly, but by scene 4 of act 3, the pace quickens, reaching a crescendo of madness and confusion that is sustained right through act 4, when temporary closure is achieved by the brief and stabilizing scene in which Sebastian follows Olivia to the altar to be wed and mistaken beginnings start to find their true conclusions. Increasingly, the pent-up energies of the play's beginning find chaotic and purgative release in physical violence, visual malapropisms, and verbal excess. Twelfth Night madness overtakes the stage and catches up the audience in its confusion. As in the third act of *King Lear*, the sense of climax is sustained by the alternation of outbursts of confusion with quieter, more constrained actions, from which we are once more propelled into the thick of the fights and mistakes that now unravel with dizzying speed. This release of theatrical energy is exhilarating, particularly since so long dammed up; but it also eventually recoils on itself. With Toby and company, we are certainly in the mood for some excellent fooling; but in the end, the jokes pile on top of one another with unnerving rapidity and lead to violence and pain. Action and language seem to veer out of control.

Ultimately, the theatrical experience of the play builds in its own corrective to our Toby-like appetites for the simple release of energy in completely unguarded and unconsidered ways. John Hollander has argued that *Twelfth Night* kills the excessive appetites of the characters by indulging them utterly. I argue that the same thing is true for certain of the spectator's theatrical appetites. We leave the third movement hungry for a theatrical and a moral norm: for action that is action, not chaos or stasis; for behavior that is neither self-regarding nor exploitative, but merely decent. After all, Twelfth Night is the *last* day of the Christmas revels, and the last day of any holiday season may leave us feeling oppressed by freedom and longing for a world of work and restraint.

Simultaneously the third movement of the play makes the audience self-regarding in yet another way. As critics of the play have shown, it is unusual in the degree to which it puts the audience in a position of superior awareness vis-à-vis the characters. We typically know more than they do in situation after situation. One figure may know more than certain others;

but we know more than any; and often a trickster in the midst of his trick unwittingly and unnervingly becomes the butt of someone else's joke. In the third movement of the plot, the events are repeatedly structured to put us in this position of superior vision. Yet so insistently is this the case, that in the end we become self-conscious about our own actual omniscience. If the characters on the stage are so wrapped in blindness, are we really more all-knowing? If they live in a world of illusions, is not the theater itself just such a world? If they rely on time and chance for illumination, do not we rely on the dramatist? If they are malleable, so are we. Within the plot, the play repeatedly gives the lie to fantasies of omnipotence and one's control of the universe. The same humbling awareness, I would argue, becomes part of the theatergoer's experience.

But let us now turn to acts 3 and 4. As I have suggested, the movement begins slowly with a sequence of short encounters between two or three characters leading up to 3.4, a scene of 300 lines in which at least twelve speaking characters appear. The events beginning this progression involve Viola and Feste, who are here alone together for the only time in the play; and their conversation has little to do with the action but much to do with the meaning of the play, since what they quibblingly discuss is the proper use of words and their easy corruption. Their conversation forms a grateful dance, in which neither strives for effect, yet both answer jest to jest with an ease that masks art and even raises Feste's resentment, since he is used to being the undisputed master of such pregnant wordplay. Viola, however, is full of admiration for the fool's skill:

> This fellow is wise enough to play the fool,
> And to do that well craves a kind of wit.
> He must observe their mood on whom he jests,
> The quality of persons, and the time;
> And, like the haggard, check at every feather
> That comes before his eye. This is a practice
> As full of labor as a wise man's art;
> For folly that he wisely shows, is fit,
> But wise men, folly-fall'n, quite taint their wit.
>
> (3.1.58–66)

The clown and heroine not only articulate a major theme of the play, the corruption of language in the mouths of those who narcissistically note only themselves and not others, but their graceful and witty dialogue also provides an example of uncorrupted speech. It establishes a normative aural ground against which the audience can hear figured subsequent deformations of that norm by those too affected, too constrained, or too egotistical to use speech with ease or to mutual benefit. Andrew's subsequent self-conscious French, "Dieu vous garde, monsieur" (69), and Viola's subsequent self-conscious compliments, "Most excellent accomplished lady, the heavens rain odors on you" (82–83), are but variations on the theme of corrupted rhetoric, though the one springs from reaching for a courtier's elegance by a man not equipped to do so and the other from Viola's false position as Orsino's go-between. Viola and Olivia fence as they have done before, not even Olivia's curt request that Viola tell her "what thou think'st of me" (135) having the power to elicit an unguarded reply from the page. Viola continues, despite Olivia's misguided declaration of love, to speak in riddles: "I am not what I am" (138). There cannot be truly open speech between them while Viola wears a man's garb, making it impossible for Olivia to "note" her truly and for her to make her denials of love convincing.

Equally at odds verbally are Toby and Andrew in the next scene, in which Toby persuades his "friend" that Olivia really loves him and will be gratified if he challenges Cesario to a duel. This is patent nonsense, and even Andrew seems at first to sense so, "'Slight! will you make an ass o' me?" (3.2.11). But Andrew hasn't enough perspicacity to note correctly the quality of Toby's friendship and too much self-love to continue long in an unflattering opinion of himself. So he allows himself to be bulldozed by Toby's coercive rhetoric. What the audience hears and sees is not plain dealing and honest interchange between friends, but a mismatch of wits and the exploitation of a foolish gull by the cruel high spirits of a master trickster. Only with the ensuing encounter between Antonio and Sebastian (3.3) does the audience once more hear language used in an unguarded, unaffected, and nonexploitative manner, the original manner of Viola talking with the sea captain on the coast of Illyria before the corruptions of disguise intervened to tangle her tongue with riddles, double meanings, and banal phrases.

The third movement of the play thus opens with a short series of aural variations, all figured against the initial ground of Viola's graceful exchanges with Feste and collectively revealing the corruption of her discourse in the mouths of those fettered by disguise, motivated by malice, or blinded by self-love, and its redemption by those who note themselves and others truly. But these three short scenes are simply the prologue to the real heart of the third movement, the frenzied scene of 375 lines that next erupts. I use the word *erupts* advisedly, because a certain tension—due to the repeated blockage of speech and action—has been building throughout the play that demands release.

On one level, of course, the story line has jockeyed a number of the characters into sterile or seemingly dead-end positions. Orsino is mooning endlessly in his palace; Malvolio is wrapped in his fantasies of being Count Malvolio; Viola is locked into man's apparel; Andrew is endlessly spending his fortune and his time in the vain pursuit of Olivia; and that lady is pining for Viola/Cesario. Clearly something has to happen to expose these false and unnatural postures and to kick these characters out of their dreamworld and release them into reality and self-knowledge. At the same time, the theater audience is ready for an emotional release. The play has been orchestrated up to this point to create a stop-and-go rhythm of stasis and partial release. Tension in the play's progressive form has largely been maintained by the aural and kinetic contrasts between adjoining scenes, but these same contrasts repeatedly suspend the movement toward climax and resolution. We are as becalmed as the characters. With 3.4 a genuine scene of climax begins to build as action increasingly takes precedence over talk and as character after character begins to reap the fruit of his or her unnatural or affected posture. As each exposes his folly in its most extreme form, the audience is set free to laugh at a world gone utterly mad, until the laughter becomes strained by our growing awareness that things are spinning out of control.

The arrival of Malvolio, yellow-stockinged and cross-gartered, sets the tone for much of the rest of the play's third movement and shows how visual malapropisms—i.e., the creation of appearances that miss their intended effect—are increasingly used to create laughter and focus attention on inappropriate behavior. Any actor worth his salt can make Malvolio's appearance hilarious. The solemn and sage steward is suddenly trying to be a young blade, straining for an effect he cannot possibly create. Locked in his egocentric world, he has no idea how his behavior seems to those around him. While he prates of greatness, Olivia marvels.

> MALVOLIO. "Be not afraid of greatness." 'Twas well writ.
> OLIVIA. What mean'st thou by that, Malvolio?
> MALVOLIO. "Some are born great."
> OLIVIA. Ha?
> MALVOLIO. "Some achieve greatness."
> OLIVIA. What say'st thou?
> MALVOLIO. "And some have greatness thrust upon them."

OLIVIA. Heaven restore thee!
MALVOLIO. "Remember who commended thy yellow
    stockings."
OLIVIA. Thy yellow stockings?
MALVOLIO. "And wished to see thee cross-gartered."
OLIVIA. Cross-gartered?
MALVOLIO. "Go to, thou art made, if thou desir'st to be so."
OLIVIA. Am I made?
MALVOLIO. "If not, let me see thee a servant still."
OLIVIA. Why, this is very midsummer madness.

                                                    (3.4.35–51)

A striking feature of the aural orchestration of this play is how often face-to-face encounters turn into contrapuntal sequences of noncommunication. Here, of course, Malvolio utterly ignores what Olivia is saying; he hears only himself, the voice of his delusions. She has her mind on her love affair, not on her steward's plight, and packs him off to be cared for by her servants and kinsman. The sequence becomes a way of registering, on the ears of the theater audience, the utter breakdown of communication in Illyria. But Shakespeare is also now quickening the pace of the action, and Malvolio no sooner struts out of sight than Andrew enters with his bizarre "challenge" for Cesario, and another joke unfolds.

In the subsequent action, Shakespeare creates a strong and complicated crescendo effect by presenting in rapid succession a series of stage actions notable for their escalating visual humor and for their increasingly strong overtones of violence. After Malvolio has modeled his lover's attire and Andrew has had his challenge read by Toby, the scene's rising action receives a momentary check as Olivia and Viola have a brief duologue of sixteen lines in which Olivia gives Viola her picture. But the momentum of the scene again surges forward, as Toby and Fabian hustle back on stage to maneuver Viola and Andrew into a duel.

Once again, visual humor is intense. At no point is the inappropriateness of Viola's male dress more comically and concretely brought home than when she is set the task of wielding a sword. Neither is the flaxen-haired Andrew much more valiant. His foolish swaggering attempts to be a good fellow all end in his craven plea that if he can avoid a duel he will give his opponent his horse. "Disguise, I see thou art a wickedness / Wherein the pregnant enemy does much" (2.2.26–27) might well be the motto for this as for surrounding scenes. On one side of the stage we see Toby pushing Andrew toward combat; on the other side Fabian doing the same for Viola.

The sight is hilarious, but also a little disconcerting. Swords are dangerous, even in comedy; and while Viola and Andrew do not seem much inclined to use them, it is hard to know where Toby's love of good sport will lead. He is not very considerate of other people's pates. Moreover, when Antonio enters and attempts to rescue Viola, we are confronted with a man who *will* use his sword and who is himself at danger in Illyria. He promptly finds himself seized by Orsino's officers and forced to reproach Viola with ingratitude for her failure to recognize him.

This interlude does not *much* distress the audience, for we now see how the plot must unravel, but it does check our laughter before the next farcical event, Sebastian's meeting with Feste, Andrew, and Toby, unfolds. The mistaking of identity is now proliferating wildly. In this new situation, both the clever Feste and the sly Toby lose their omniscience. Neither can note truly the person before him, and the pranksters nearly get roundly thrashed before Olivia's fortuitous entry calms the escalating violence. We have seen, in succession, Malvolio duped by a plot into behaving like an ass before Olivia; Olivia deceived by Viola's disguise into offering her picture as a love gift; Viola and Andrew manipulated by lies and their own false advertising of self into a duel neither wants; Antonio deceived by Viola's clothes into believing she is his friend; and Toby and company deceived by Sebastian's clothes into believing he is the duke's cowardly messenger. The consequences of these mistakes become increasingly dangerous. No one seems to know anything for certain; all confident assumptions prove illusions—a thought that cannot but bring pressure to bear upon the audience's own comfortable feelings of omniscience. When will we too be duped? What are the constraints upon our vision and power?

But even at this point, when the madness on the stage would seem to have been played out fully and when our appetite for action has been well satisfied, we find out that this frenzied movement of the play has not reached its conclusion. One more fillip remains, one more change to be rung on the theme of madness and disguise, and that is provided by the revelation of the imprisoned Malvolio and the sight of Feste capering about as Sir Topas. The steward, who never really would listen to anybody, now is desperate to have someone listen to him. He truly is in the dark hole created by his own ignorance and pomposity; and Feste, now as the fool, now as Sir Topas, gives him a dose of his own medicine: lets him see how it is to be snubbed and disregarded by those who for the moment have power. But this scene is delicately handled. It is both the culmination of the farcical madness that has overtaken the stage for several scenes and the clearest signal of its impending collapse.

Disguise has, by this point in the play, become a major visual motif; and events in the drama's third movement have increasingly linked disguise with violence and confusion. It is unsettling to the audience, then, when Feste gratuitously assumes the disguise of a curate—as Maria notes, Malvolio can't *see* Feste, so his robes are for our benefit, not the steward's. Attired thus, Feste assumes several voices in succession and breaks out in manic song as he harasses the hapless steward. This is funny, but it is also the capstone of the protean shape-changing and assumption of false roles that have already caused so much trouble in Illyria. One need not sentimentalize Malvolio's plight—he richly deserves a comeuppance—to feel that events are rolling out of control. Feste's final song, equating himself with Vice of the morality plays and Malvolio with the devil, suggests the extent to which the world has been turned on its head and order threatened. It is thus with relief that the audience hears Feste promise to bring Malvolio a pen and paper, and sees in the next scene Sebastian enter by himself and decide on an action that seems both natural and right. He is going to wed Olivia. In this topsy-turvy world, at least one Jack and Jill are going to make it to the altar.

By now the audience is quite ready for less madness. Action we have had in abundance and also emotional release through laughter. But the mistakes and the misperceptions have almost ceased to be funny. We are reeling from the pace of events and sensitive—because of the repeated undermining of each character's fix on reality and because wished-for events have snowballed almost beyond the point at which we can take pleasure in them—to our dependence upon the dramatist for the security of our perceptions and the control of our pleasure and pain.

What remains is the effecting of theatrical closure and the establishment of theatrical and moral equilibrium after the severe disturbance of both. The fourth movement of the play does just that. It brings illumination to the characters through release from disguises of every stripe, and it brings the theater event to a poised, if tenuous conclusion, as linguistic and kinetic energy find expression in a scene that is both energetic and highly patterned. In fact, 5.1 is probably the most schematically orchestrated scene of the entire play. And it must be. A great deal happens in it, but the happenings do not spin out of control. Watching the scene, we feel, what we so rarely feel in life, the perfect marriage of energy and restraint. The final movement of the play is four hundred lines long and falls into two distinct parts with the turn marked very precisely by Sebastian's final entry. Up to that point what is remarkable is the way in which Shakespeare orchestrates aural and visual events to create for a final time the sensation of impasse and frustration that results from mistakes of identity and the assumption of unnatural poses. One by one characters who have otherwise not shared a stage together assemble in one place, but their coming together at first does not result in the harmony one would expect.

The scene begins promisingly, however. The first striking event is the sight of Orsino walking the streets of Illyria and not holed up in his palace. We have come to expect that we will see him isolated from the world, listening to lugubrious music, and lamenting his unrequited love. It is a visual surprise, therefore, to observe him in the open air bantering with Feste and moving toward Olivia's. This visual cue signals that his claustrophobic self-imprisonment may be over. There is, furthermore, relief in seeing Feste once more in his characteristic role of fool, begging for money, and no longer disguised as a curate.

But as more characters enter—the visual crescendo underscoring a rising sense of anticipation—language once more becomes hopelessly entangled. Characters have so long pretended to be what they are not that, even when they genuinely try to communicate, they still speak at cross purposes. Each successive entrance merely compounds the confusion of identities, and questions fly thick and fast with few satisfying answers given. Antonio is clearly revealed as Orsino's old enemy, but he *seems* to be lying about his rescue of Viola. Olivia makes clear her love for Cesario, but either she or Viola *seems* to be lying about the wedding that is supposed to have occurred. Toby and Andrew clearly have taken a drubbing in a duel, but either they or Viola *seems* to be lying about who gave them that drubbing.

Only when Sebastian enters can misunderstandings be resolved. His opening lines make plain that it was he who beat Toby and wed Olivia. "I am sorry, madam, I have hurt your kinsman" (5.1.201). A moment later he also redeems Antonio from the imputation of a lie by acknowledging him as his rescuer. Paradoxically, it is a visual image of doubleness, two identically dressed twins, that "natural perspective" of which Orsino speaks, that allows simple and single truth to emerge. Now there are more questions; but, like the satisfying ritualistic questions of the catechism, they have answers:

> SEBASTIAN. Of charity, what kin are you to me?
>   What countryman? What name? What parentage?
> VIOLA. Of Messaline; Sebastian was my father;
>   Such a Sebastian was my brother too.
>
>   (5.1.222–25)

Students with a penchant for realism often object that it takes the twins an unconscionably long time to recognize one another. But, of course, realism is not the point. The point is that the tick-tock of question and answer, detail countered with confirming detail, is part of a ritual of recognition, a way of redeeming the self and language from the confusion into which both have fallen. And it is a theatrically necessary ritual, fulfilling a desire for direct, open, and reciprocated speech that has been frustrated for five acts. After the unanswered questions of the first half of the scene, the answered questions of Sebastian and Viola give special pleasure to characters and audience alike. Through them, characters find release from the prison of disguise and affectation in which they long have been locked. Orsino can now note Viola and her selfless service truly; Olivia, her "extracting frenzy" (273) past, can remember her servant Malvolio and note his letter truly. Only he, vowing revenge on the "lighter people" (329), cannot move from his dark and claustrophobic pride to accept what he is and the lessons the mad time of confusion has brought to light.

As the play ends, nearly all the characters stand before us released from their egocentricity and disguises. They possess knowledge only we, the audience, had previously possessed; and with that knowledge comes the humbling realization that many prior assumptions were wrong. Orsino was wrong about his love for Olivia; Andrew was mistaken about Toby's friendship; Olivia was misled in her belief that Cesario was a man; and Antonio was mistaken about Sebastian's ingratitude. Now, in each instance, the truth stands revealed.

Of course, not everything in the Illyrian world is perfect; and the harmony achieved by play's end is notably tenuous. Malvolio, for example, is still angry; Antonio is never officially pardoned; Andrew does not find a love that is requited; and Orsino is insistent that Viola return to her maiden weeds before he embraces her and then promises she will be his "mistress and his fancy's queen" (377), a phrase that sounds rather too much like his earlier idealization of Olivia. Nonetheless, though these details qualify the impression of harmony that marks the play's final moments, they cannot erase it. Most poses have been banished, and the characters are given the opportunity to grow beyond their prior selves.

But the audience's experience is not over yet. It, too, must be released from the role of spectator and from the manipulations of the dramatist. For the spectator this release is effected by Feste's song. As the play began in music, so it ends in music. But the closing song is neither a mournful love lyric nor a high-spirited catch; it is simply a song sung by an aging clown about the frustrations and disappointments of living. This song is not self-pitying, but it *is* melancholy and resigned. It ushers the audience from the heightened world of Illyria, where many characters now seem poised to embrace a golden peace, back to a world in which "the rain it raineth every day," the world of our daily lives.

During the course of the play, we have become aware of our dependence on the dramatist; but his control has proved to be, after all, a benign control, an echo, perhaps of that providential power which wafted Sebastian to Illyria. The playwright has manipulated us and made us aware of that manipulation, but he has neither misled us (as he was later to do in *The Winter's Tale*, where for three acts we believe Hermione is dead when in truth she lives) nor cheated us of the happy ending we desire, though he has hedged that ending with qualifications that suggest how easily our desires could have been frustrated. More strikingly, by the way Shakespeare finally releases the audience from the play, he reminds us that, in the world beyond the theater, the forces which govern our experience are often less benign than the dramatist of *Twelfth Night* has been. Outside the theater, we are the pawns of time and chance, not the creatures of a generous playwright. And time and chance, while they sometimes bring ships safely to port, also bring pain, alienation, and frustration of desire. Feste's song, with its haunting refrain about the wind and the rain, is a chastening reminder of this truth and an important part of our experience of *Twelfth Night*.

The prior analysis has moved—progressively and, of course, too swiftly—through *Twelfth Night* to suggest in broad outlines how Shakespeare orchestrates the theatrical event to make the themes and the ideas of the play part of the audience's theatrical experience. My assumption here and throughout [*Shakespeare's Art of Orchestration*] has been that the theatrical experience is both a cerebral and a sensory one, and that it is impossible to separate the two. My *emphasis* has been, however, on what is too often neglected in dramatic criticism: the orchestration of the sensory components of the implied performance as a means of guiding audience perceptions and shaping responses as the dramatic event unfolds in time.

In *Twelfth Night* Shakespeare constantly uses aural and visual cues to foreground particular events and to call attention to key motifs: disguise, corrupted language, affectation. And, as I have suggested, even the kinetic aspects of our experience of the play—our involvement in its rhythms of restraint and release—become integral to our understanding of what the play is about and to an understanding, finally, of its moral vision. We know the enervating consequences of false poses and self-indulgent egotism because we have felt their effects in the blocked actions, the contorted speeches, and the contrapuntal dialogues of noncommunication that repeatedly punctuate the play and make its theatrical course turn aside and lose the name of action.

The play is crafted to tamper with the satisfaction of some very basic theatrical appetites—a desire for movement, happening, clear speeches eventuating in insight and action. By stifling action and thwarting purposeful speech, the play creates an impatience based initially on theatrical frustration and then transmuted into moral anger; into impatience with the disguises, pomposity, and self-centeredness that create the stasis and sense of entrapment in the world of the play and that we feel in the theater as pent-up kinetic energy begging for release. As in *Hamlet*, another play of thwarted theatrical energies, impatience for a time may make us root for the brutal simplicities of a Toby (benign cousin of Claudius), fertile engineer of plots and actions of all sorts, before we come to recognize in the play's climactic third movement the insufficiencies of pure action undertaken without regard for its effects and human consequences. Moreover, the tension in the Illyrian world between human will as the shaper of human destiny and the power of time and chance resonates with the audience's own awareness of the dramatist's hand in establishing the parameters of its own perception and responses. In this most sophisticated of comedies, men are free and not free; the same thing may be said of the theatergoer.

In short, Shakespeare finds in *Twelfth Night*, as in all his plays, a very specific theatrical vocabulary by which the enacted script communicates with its audience. This is a vocabulary, not just of words, but also of gestures, sounds, images, and movements that are woven together to create theatrical events of great complexity. In orchestrating these sensory elements of the implied performance, Shakespeare always keeps one eye on the audience. The full dramatic meaning of his works is realized only in our responses to them. In [*Shakespeare's Art of Orchestration*] I have examined some of the ways in which this interaction between play and audience is shaped: how Shakespeare's techniques of orchestration form a repertoire of performance strategies aimed at the full participation of the theatergoer in the dramatic event and his actualization of its meaning. That Shakespeare's art of orchestration is purposeful and complex I hope I have shown; that it is effective is proven daily in the theaters of the world.

Shakespeare's Realism: Viola

Gary Taylor

"The real" may be imagined as a sphere: that is, a polygon of an infinite number of sides. (Of course, as the concept of infinity is itself a mathematical fiction, I am here defining reality in terms of fiction.) From among this multiplicity of aspects, each artist selects a few, which and how many according to his talents and his times. All art is synecdoche. Naturalist playwrights have elevated into law a handful of the more mechanical aspects of the real. Theirs is a realism by contagion: a figure sitting in a real chair smoking real cigarettes must himself be real. The naturalists reinforce the reality of the actor's presence with the reality of his stage environment. But the set merely persists; after its initial assertion, it fades from our attention, it becomes truly redundant (in the pejorative sense). This is the bombast of naturalism, its inflated insistence upon a reality spectators are only too willing to concede—up to a point. Beyond that point the rhetoric of chairs and cigarettes cannot persuade us to go; it cannot prevent our remembering it's only a play; it cannot forestall our seeing the rabbit as well as the duck. Art is not life. The painter's materials are only two-dimensional; the sculptor's materials cannot move; the play cannot last a lifetime, and yet, for so long as it does last, it must secure the attention of its audience. The artist compensates as he can for the limits of his material, foreshortening lines, polishing stone flesh, contorting time. Shakespeare creates by the marshalling of combinations in time, so that at any moment the brilliance of one quality obscures the absence of another. Naturalists therefore find it won-

---

From *To Analyze Delight: A Hedonist Criticism of Shakespeare.* © 1985 by Gary Taylor. University of Delaware Press, 1985.

derfully easy and gratifying to reveal contradictions, silly conventions, artifice of motive and timing and language. They find it less easy to explain
why Shakespeare's fictions convince, more than their own.

The other characters describe Viola for us. They allude thirty-two
times to her youth. Less frequently but more emphatically, Orsino and
Olivia and Sebastian praise her for physical beauty. They mention also,
though in passing and only half a dozen times, her wit, her eloquence, her
intelligence—but, as they do not so finely demarcate the boundaries between these qualities, we might as well lump them all under Wit (which
was, in any case, a more comprehensive term in Shakespeare's day than it is
in ours). The Captain calls her a lady, or "madam," and thereafter in
disguise she is a gentleman, insistently and to all. No one says any more
than this. This is a Viola pretty, witty and well-off, but little else. Of these
attributes, we would call only her wit a character trait, and even that we see
for ourselves, which makes description redundant. The others—age, looks,
status—would besides be obvious to an audience at a glance. Why then
burden the play with vague and useless adjectives?

Since for most of the play Viola dresses and acts as a servant, we must
be reminded that her true nobility makes her a fit match for the Duke, and
that her subservience to him reflects choice, not birth or social need. For
most of the play too she is a man, therefore we must be told how beautiful
she is. Youth must be stressed because her disguise depends on it; because
some characters who do not know her name must speak of her; because the
word's sexual neutrality lets us think of her as female when they address her
as a male; because youth belongs to the Petrarchan ensemble of beauty, wit,
virtue and money. All these traits, so cheerfully shallow, are simple panegyric, and, like the immediate and deep affection she inspires in the Captain, Orsino, Olivia and Sebastian, they prejudice us in her favour, they
ensure our emotional allegiance.

But there are men and women, members of audiences, who cannot
forgive others money or eloquence or innocence or a fortunate face. Malvolio and Olivia call Viola's wit rude, Toby calls her a coward, Antonio an
ingrate, and the final scene heaps calumny on her. These opinions are variously discredited. Malvolio's distaste for her follows his diatribe against
Feste, which earned him Olivia's rebuke; wit is usually thought rude by its
victims; Viola only does what Orsino ordered, even repeating his metaphor. Olivia, who first dislikes the messenger for the master's sake, soon
more than compensates by falling in love with him (her). The later accusations are all misunderstandings. When alone with Fabian, Toby praises her,
so that his criticisms afterward belong to the gulling of Aguecheek. Viola's
generosity and gratitude the play dramatizes repeatedly and early, as though

expressly to anticipate Antonio's intense but mistaken charge. Besides, Viola does give him half she has. Even if the accusations of cowardice were justified, cowardice was and probably still is judged forgivable in a woman, especially a young one. The Viola they call coward faces death at Orsino's hands "most jocund, apt, and willingly." Shakespeare thus broaches Viola's faults only in contexts which discredit criticism, reserving the bulk of it for her last scenes, by which time our allegiance is secure. But he does broach faults. In bodying an ideal (as Viola is), decoys must be planted for cynicism, so that it wastes itself on trifles; otherwise it wells up against the whole. Viola is an inkblot, which various minds on stage interpret variously. We read them by how they read her. And the flux of their opinions looks likelier than massed choruses of unchanging praise and suspect unanimity.

These are qualities peripheral and narrative. Critics have put such stress on commentary of this kind, on the testimony of other characters, only because it seems a way to simplify the task of interpretation. But we do not take Viola on hearsay: we see her ourselves, before anyone has a chance to talk of her, or tell us what to think. We experience her ourselves, mostly through her own words. But of Viola's many sins against realism, we in this century are perhaps most sensitive to her unnatural mouth.

> Mine own escape unfoldeth to my hope,
> Whereto thy speech serves for authority,
> The like of him.

No one talks like that. Shakespeare nevertheless was and is admired for capturing the form of speech and the particulars of a voice, and I do not think it rash to assume there is some reason for the praise.

Viola begins in the fourth line of her first scene a digression, a parenthesis seventeen lines long, about her brother.

> And what should I do in Illyria?
> My brother he is in Elysium.
> Perchance he is not drowned. What think you, sailors?

The digression begins almost imperceptibly, suggested by association of sound and situation, and the contrast between herself arriving on this shore and her brother arriving on another and stranger shore. But a digression it remains, as can be seen by cutting lines 3–23 of the scene.

> What country, friends, is this?

> Know'st thou this country?

> Who governs here?
>
> What is his name?
>
> He was a bachelor then.
>
> What's she?

A real Viola might in fact ask uninterrupted just such a string of questions. But to an audience, if "the tenour of the dialogue" seems too governed by a goal, that goal can easily look like the playwright's not the character's, because the audience knows the playwright must get through his exposition, and because conversation as commonly practised is seldom linear or directed: each party to the dialogue steers a different course, while even within a single mind cross purposes compete for mastery and expression. Speakers are interrupted, or interrupt themselves. The tacks conversation takes thus serve the revelation of mind, the contrasts of purpose between and within minds. Viola begins, detours, begins again, putting parentheses within parentheses: from Illyria to Elysium, to the thought that perhaps her brother is not drowned after all, to asking the sailors for their opinion, to the Captain's cautious reply, to Viola's exclamation "O my poor brother!" which responds to the Captain's caution by assuming the worst, before she reverts to the comfort of "perchance," making the best of the Captain's reply. Indeed, up to the mention of Orsino, the entire dialogue is structurally parenthetic, as it exists without relation to what goes before. It thus seems unattached and free, and, though eventually it submits to its place in the plot, that cannot diminish the freedom we feel meanwhile.

These and other digressions overlapping and in concert obscure an otherwise naked exposition. The scene must tell what it did and what will happen, and without Viola's false start it breaks in two: the past in one package, the future in another. Arthur Miller called "how to dramatize what has gone before" "the biggest single dramatic problem." Shakespeare did not think so: he gives almost nothing of the past (which partly explains the frustrations of psychoanalytic criticism). We are informed of Viola's immediate past incidentally, through the Captain's narration of Sebastian's. Shakespeare does not bother over Viola's name, or where she came from, or her motives for coming or for disguising herself, or the other helps John Kemble was happy to supply:

> Thou shalt present me as a page unto him,
> Of gentle breeding, and my name Cesario:—
> This trunk, the reliques of my sea-drown'd brother,
> Will furnish man's apparel to my need.

Here Shakespeare does not (as he did in the first scene of *The Comedy of Errors*) spoonfeed us facts. Instead, just when other playwrights are scrambling to piece together a plot, he drops morsels of a time distant and gratuitous, unelaborated, obviously not summoned up for the plot's sake, but again intimating discreetly life outside the play's limits. And these particulars are not only delightful or intriguing in themselves, but positively distract us from a consciousness of the exposition.

> Ay madam, well, for I was bred and born
> Not three hours' travel from this very place.

> Orsino! I have heard my father name him.
> He was a bachelor then.

This last line cues, naturally enough, the Captain's mention of Olivia. Orsino is not named till now, and, though we may suspect he is the Duke in question, until they link him to Olivia we cannot be sure. But Olivia is a dead end. The talk of her comes to nothing, as much talk does. Afterwards begins another parenthesis, this one with no immediate relation whatever to the preceding dialogue.

> There is a fair behaviour in thee, Captain,
> And though that nature with a beauteous wall
> Doth oft close in pollution, yet of thee
> I will believe thou hast a mind that suits
> With this thy fair and outward character.

Only as she continues does the relevance of this panegyric become apparent.

> I prithee—and I'll pay thee bounteously—
> Conceal me what I am, and be my aid.

The talk of Olivia turns out not to have been wasted after all, and, since Viola must convince the Captain to act for her, exposition of her plans seems here necessary and natural. Her praise of the Captain is thus motivated in retrospect.

In her next scene, she and Orsino discuss Olivia without once naming her, referring to her simply by pronouns, leaving the identification to our intelligence. Viola and Olivia in their first encounter answer questions with questions, speak at cross purposes, Olivia testing hypotheses about the intruder; Maria interrupts them; Olivia interrupts Viola; the message is never delivered.

> OLIVIA. If I do not usurp myself, I am.
> VIOLA. Most certain, if you are she, you do usurp yourself, for
>   what is yours to bestow is not yours to reserve.

The nature of wit is to digress, to pounce upon peripherals and explode them into prominence.

> OLIVIA. Were you sent hither to praise me?
> VIOLA. I see you what you are: you are too proud.
> But if you were the devil, you are fair.
> My lord and master loves you. O, such love
> Could be but recompens'd, though you were crown'd
> The nonpareil of beauty!

Viola does not answer Olivia's question, but judges it, as an expression of pride (the devil's own sin). But Olivia is beautiful, and so has cause for pride—except that beauty, however great, could never deserve more than the kind of love which Orsino offers.

The technique is everywhere much the same, employing a variation or postponement of the expected sequence. The pattern and quantity of such digression varies according to the number and complexity of the partici-pants. But the discontinuities never become obtrusive, as they do in the mannerist dialogue of Pinter and Mamet: the quantity or incongruity of the diversions does not lead an audience to generalize that the eccentricities of individual consciousness forbid any possibility of communication. Instead, the norm of directed and interacting conversation highlights occasional changes of course, which seem as a result to reveal the particular internal pressures of an individual personality. Moreover, the impression of natural speech derives not only from the deployment of sentences in a natural haphazard, but from the sentences themselves.

> Know'st thou this country?
>
> Who governs here?
>
> What is his name?
>
> Orsino! I have heard my father name him.
>
> He was a bachelor then.
>
> What's she?
>
> I'll serve this duke.
>
> I thank thee. Lead me on.
>
> I thank you. Here comes the count.
>
> Say I do speak to her, my lord, what then?

I'll do my best to woo your lady.

Good madam, let me see your face.

I left no ring with her.

She loves me, sure.

None of my lord's ring? Why, he sent her none.

How will this fadge?

What will become of this?

But if she cannot love you, sir?

(Save you, gentleman.)—And you, sir.

I pity you.

(Gentleman, God save thee)— And you, sir.

I am no fighter.

Pray you, sir, do you know of this matter?

I beseech you, what manner of man is he?

Pray sir, put your sword up, if you please.

What money, sir?

He nam'd Sebastian.

Why do you speak to me? I never hurt you.

Of Messaline: Sebastian was my father.

My father had a mole upon his brow.

These are natural enough. But my singling out of these does not imply that elsewhere Viola's every word proclaims itself poetry and made not born. The proportion of art to nature varies from line to line.

> Say that some lady, as perhaps there is,
> Hath for your love as great a pang of heart
> As you have for Olivia; you cannot love her;
> You tell her so. Must she not then be answer'd?

Here only "pang of heart" and the displacement of the preposition "for your love," between the verb and its object, seem literary. To modern ears "hath" sounds archaic and "poetic," but though "has" was displacing it even in Shakespeare's lifetime, its literary flavour must have been much weaker than now. "Then" would probably seem more natural at the beginning or end of the question, although this might be challenged—especially because, as its position is right metrically, any slight syntactical dislocation tends to be erased. Meter and syntax give us two competing definitions of "rightness," which can in such marginal cases be used interchangeably. For instance, in "What country, friends, is this?" only the displacement of the vocative suggests the written not the spoken word, and meter tends to obscure this—as does our own familiarity with the line. (Familiarity is as important as changes in linguistic usage in obscuring for us the exact feel of much of Shakespeare's dialogue.)

The lilt of speech can be found in varying amounts everywhere in the poetry. But again, this balancing and map of words is perpetual, and so to analyse its relation to character we must isolate Viola's wholly natural and unadulterated lines from the rest. The list is small, but its items are surprisingly prominent: "Good madam, let me see your face" (because it is a non sequitur, because Viola here changes from a passive to an active role in the dialogue of 1.5, because we know what motivates the change); "I left no ring with her" (her first bewildered response, alone after Malvolio's exit in 2.2, to the second major irony of the plot); "I pity you" (her only reply to Olivia's tortuous long confession in 3.1); "Pray sir, put your sword up, if you please" (her small voice after the hubbub between Antonio, Sir Toby, and Fabian in 3.4—the more remarkable for its contrast with Antonio's "Put up your sword!"); "What money, sir?" (her first words to Antonio after his repeated requests, in the play's first mistaking of brother and sister); "Of Messaline: Sebastian was my father" (her first words to Sebastian after his string of vocatives, tantalizing us with the expectation of "Sebastian was my brother," in the moment of recognition to which the whole play leads, and which lends its power to her next lone sentence too); "My father had a mole upon his brow."

These examples owe their emphasis to their contexts, contexts in which stylized or poetic language would be as or almost as emphatic, but elsewhere Viola's plainness stands out simply because it's plain.

> *For saying so, there's gold.*
> Mine own escape unfoldeth to my hope,
> Whereto thy speech serves for authority,
> The like of him. *Know'st thou this country?*

> Most radiant, exquisite and unmatchable

> beauty—*I pray you tell me if this be the*
> *lady of the house.*

ORSINO. Tell her my love, more noble than the world,
    Prizes not quantity of dirty lands;
    The parts that fortune hath bestow'd upon her,
    Tell her I hold as giddily as fortune;
    But 'tis that miracle and queen of gems
    That nature pranks her in, attracts my soul.
VIOLA. *But if she cannot love you, sir?*

Such collisions of style advertise each. Unrelieved naturalism is inconspicuous because constant; Shakespeare's is strategic realism.

In achieving for Viola this impression of artless speech, Shakespeare employs sentences with no great complexity of syntax or rhetoric or vocabulary. But he also employs little or no slang, or interjection, or commonplace, or imagery of everyday life, nothing bathetic or trite, no repetition of unmeaning social formulae (though Olivia so interprets Viola's claim to be her "servant'). Judged by this progress of negatives, Viola may well seem less real than Sir Toby—which is only to say his reality is the more easily explained. In fact, Toby's easy coexistence with Viola itself lends her life: the differences between them thus seem less the gap between natural and manufactured than the variety and distinction of two reals. The means used to enliven each fiction will themselves individuate it. What they are proves that they are. We know Viola partly by what she's not, by all the kinds of language she does not use. The vocabulary she does use is unphysical (notoriously chaste), often latinate and polysyllabic, often abstract, with a preference for verbal nouns ("my having is not much"), substantives and personifications, and for a balanced syntax making analytical distinctions ("what is yours to bestow is not yours to reserve"). What imagery she has tends to the conventional and consciously poetic ("Elysium"), to comparisons so familiar they need only be implied.

> 'Tis beauty truly blent, whose red and white
> Nature's own sweet and cunning hand laid on.

Such sunken imagery suggests an unassertive elegance.

Character is repetition: repetitions of speech, as we have seen, but also repetitions of action. Viola expresses her gratitude to the Captain, to Valentine, to Fabian and then Antonio, to Antonio again in the last scene. "I hate ingratitude more in a man / Than lying, vainness, babbling drunkenness." She offers money to the Captain twice, to Feste twice; she gives Antonio half she has. She often has occasion for gratitude and generosity, because she depends often on others: the Captain, Valentine, Olivia, Feste, Fabian, Toby, Antonio. Though she knows more than any other character on stage, she is forever in the position of having to ask others questions. Helpless herself, she trusts to time. Repeatedly and at length she praises others, especially Olivia, Feste and the Captain. She feels for her brother, for Olivia, Antonio and Orsino; typically, even her love she expresses as sympathy for someone else, either Orsino or a "sister." She does describe Malvolio as a "churlish messenger" (2.2), and does wish Olivia ill luck in love (1.5)—this is the most malice she can muster, and she soon regrets cursing Olivia. Despite (or because of) her own social rank, respect and courtesy—"my lord," "my lady," "sir"—are always on her lips. Unlike Petrarchan women, she honours and obeys her husband *before* marriage, serving him in the most selfless manner imaginable, and is literally his servant when metaphorically he should be hers. She doubts her own abilities, a modesty which extends to things sexual: of all Shakespeare's comic heroines, Viola has the most chaste mouth and mind. But, like them all, she is practical and persistent. Circumstance does not permit her the luxuries of grief for her brother; she understands better than Orsino how futile his romance diplomacy is; she will not let Malvolio's excuses or Olivia's questions or Maria's interruption deflect her from her business; she does not let despair canker her love. She shows her wit off stage with Malvolio, on stage with Olivia, Maria, Feste and Toby; she shows her intelligence in deducing Olivia's love and Antonio's mistake.

What this list brings together the play disperses, so that we are seldom conscious of repetition. Viola's redistribution of wealth—of all her repetitions the one most physical, and thus most prone to look mechanical—is carefully varied. She first gives, then only promises, the Captain money (1.2); Feste wittily begs for what she gave the Captain unasked (3.1); Antonio passionately demands money, she only offers him half, he refuses it (3.4); Viola herself refuses a fee from Olivia (1.5). Others remark upon her wit, and that she hates ingratitude she says herself, but the other repetitions pass without comment, and are so subtly interfused I do them violence by disentangling them. Generosity is financial gratitude; praise turns to gratitude, sympathy turns to praise. That sympathy itself blends into her own sorrows for her brother's death and her unanswered love. Her sorrow is reticent and practical; her wit persistent; her reticence patient; her love sorrowing. Her self-doubts naturally spring from helplessness and naturally contribute to her reticence and passivity.

We need never conceptualize her aspects in this way; Shakespeare himself need not have. But this interrelation of traits is what allows the character to assimilate new material. For instance, in the duel with Aguecheek, if Viola is petrified with fear, her cowardice will seem in character, because related to her helplessness, reticence and passivity. We have already had occasion to laugh, when her disguise entangles her in absurd difficulties, and we will laugh now at her helpless perplexity. But, equally, if Viola soundly thrashes Aguecheek—as some actresses have done—that too will seem in character, by analogy with her practicality, her persistence, her repeatedly demonstrated ability to better her opponents (of whom Aguecheek is no doubt the least daunting). If she decides the fight cannot be avoided, then she must do her best, and she will no doubt be surprised and delighted by her own success.

Viola then is a system of repetitions—descriptions repeated, patterns of speech and action repeated—repetitions varied and intertwined, authenticated by natural speech, authenticated too by the presence of other characters defined by different patterns of repetition. It has long been recognized that, in M. C. Bradbrook's words, "Romeo and Juliet without the Nurse and Mercutio, Navarre and his lords without Armado, Costard, Moth and the worthies, Richard without Bolingbroke, York, Gaunt and the Queen, would in effect cease to exist with the dramatic depth and significance which makes them what they are." Richard and Bolinbroke define each other dialectically, as do Creon and Antigone. But such oppositions, though they have naturally attracted critical attention, are not the only, or even the normal, method of distinguishing and relating character. Olivia and Viola are not alike, and to that extent each defines the other by opposition, but they are never offered as dialectical alternatives, and in fact Olivia might easily seem too like Viola, both being highborn women, both in love, both unrequited, both mourning a brother. The individuality of the two impresses us partly because (as with Jane Austen's six clergymen) in outline they are so similar.

Olivia commands; Viola entreats and obeys. Olivia in her first scene criticizes Feste, Malvolio, Sir Toby and Viola; she gives sermons and expresses curt moral disapproval. Viola praises. Olivia shows Orsino no sympathy; Viola sympathizes even with Olivia, her rival. Olivia is proud, and told so; her anticipation of praise is all the more striking after Viola's silence during Orsino's praise, in the preceding scene. And, though Olivia has on the whole a ladylike vocabulary, she does not have Viola's latinity, and is occasionally capable of "bird-bolts," "rudesby," "fat and fulsome howling," "inventories," "utensils," "lids for pans," of "What ho!" "Fie on him!" and "Go to." She mocks conventional imagery. She describes her own love violently:

> Even so quickly may one catch the plague!

> Have you not set mine honour at the stake,
> And baited it with all th'unmuzzled thoughts
> That tyrannous heart can think?

> A murd'rous guilt shows not itself more soon
> Than love that would be hid.

> A fiend like thee might bear my soul to hell.

Viola in love waits and is silent; Olivia acts, and openly, confessing her love, persisting, calling Cesario back, hurrying Sebastian to a priest. Viola first communicates her feelings in an unelaborated aside, Olivia in a long soliloquy, full of exclamations, repetitions, headstrong images. And, unlike Viola, she does not mourn her brother long, or feelingly. Admittedly, Sebastian can be resurrected at play's end (as Olivia's brother cannot), and Viola may in the meantime intensely communicate her loss without unbalancing the comedy. Viola's grief directly contributes to the joy of the denouement, as Olivia's could not. Admittedly also, Viola does not recall her own grief in Olivia's company, and no one speaks of Olivia's brother after act 1, which is to say Shakespeare does not focus moral disapproval, or demand comparison, as he easily could. Stressing Olivia's broken vow, when she falls in love and gives up mourning, would make a situation already complex and painful even more so. But, still, Olivia must either cease to wear black early in the play, and so physically announce an end to grief, or by continuing in black invite a contrast between her clothes and her thoughts, which are by now oblivious to her brother. Viola's grief impresses us as central; Olivia's never does. Her vow is instead a typical expression of her will, and a (conscious or unconscious) defence against Orsino.

Olivia also abhors yellow. No one need extrapolate conclusions from such differences; no one need notice them; but imperceptibly the impressions accumulate, and being imperceptible they seem the more real, they seem like life, and unlike characters demarcated by their opinions on this and that. We know Viola is not Olivia, but do not know quite why or how we know—though, if asked, we could begin to formulate and conceptualize distinctions. Our experience of human beings leads us to expect variety and individuality. If one actress stands before us on the stage, her reality is proven by her presence; but if another enters we shall expect not only reality but also distinction. Of course, they may share many traits, but, as the actresses must now convince us they represent two different persons, their own vitality is no longer sufficient for the illusion. But, though we require differentiation, the differences need not *mean* anything, any more than the difference between apples and pears means anything, though we might expect a still life to distinguish them. Such variety becomes a condition for our assent. But the variety itself gives us pleasure, too, by perpetually supplying fresh sources of interest, new claims on our attention.

Other characters invite other contrasts. Orsino's language is intense, inventive, polysyllabic, self-conscious, complex and metaphorical, without Viola's lucidity or simplicity, and as if to emphasize this contrast Viola is at her most reticent in his company: in their first scene together (1.5), she speaks seven lines to his twenty-four. He speaks of his love loudly and at large, and seems to relish his pain as a proof of sincerity.

> There is no woman's sides
> Can bide the beating of so strong a passion
> As love doth give my heart; no woman's heart
> So big, to hold so much. They lack retention.
> Alas, their love may be called appetite:
> No motion of the liver, but the palate,
> That suffer surfeit, cloyment, and revolt.
> But mine is all as hungry as the sea
> And can digest as much. Make no compare
> Between that love a woman can bear me
> And that I owe Olivia.

If his sorrows do not touch us as Viola's do, that is perhaps because he pities himself enough for us all, and because the very beauty of his poetry impersonalizes it, distracting our attention from the man to the phrase.

Sebastian grows rapidly exasperated then angry at the very misunderstandings Viola suffers comically; when brother and sister meet, he expresses wonder and plain-faced astonishment, she quietly and surely reveals herself, savouring and drawing out their reunion:

> SEBASTIAN. Do I stand there? I never had a brother,
> Nor can there be that deity in my nature
> Of here and everywhere. I had a sister,
> Whom the blind waves and surges have devour'd.

> Of charity, what kin are you to me?
> What countryman? What name? What parentage?
> VIOLA. Of Messaline; Sebastian was my father.
> Such a Sebastian was my brother, too;
> So went he suited to his watery tomb.
> If spirits can assume both form and suit,
> You come to fright us.

When he turns to Olivia and offers her himself, Viola does not speak, but waits for Orsino.

Unlike Malvolio, Viola does not misinterpret Orsino's actions according to her own vanity, or deceive herself into confidence. Malvolio is an aspirant lord; Viola willingly and without complaint humbles herself to service. Malvolio is an unnecessarily churlish messenger; Viola, having excellent reasons to misdeliver the message, speaks it as passionately as she can.

To Viola's characterization Aguecheek, Toby, Fabian, Maria and Feste all contribute one contrast, an attitude to money, sex, food, drink, fighting, singing, manners, life—a contrast which also defines Olivia and Orsino, though to varying degrees. It is perhaps most easily defined as a class contrast, though it disregards class boundaries. Feste sings for Toby and Aguecheek in 2.3, then for Orsino and Viola in the next scene, thus juxtaposing the leisure amusements of the two sets; Maria and Toby plot the discomfiting of Malvolio just after Viola in soliloquy decides, after Malvolio leaves, to continue her disguise, in sympathy for all and at some cost to herself. Feste's perpetual begging and the financial tie of Toby and Aguecheek illuminate Viola's generosity; duelling as a practical joke shows up her peaceable nature. She crushes Aguecheek's pretensions to culture and Toby's to eloquence. But she does not morally condemn them. She will pun with Feste, bawdily too, without objecting to his indecencies, and she does not blame anyone for wanting money, though she does not want it herself and feels insulted by mercenary treatment. She praises Feste's singing and fooling just as Toby and Aguecheek do. Though in the duel Aguecheek and she may both be dupes, he has contributed to his own confounding, while she is pure victim; though she may be as cowardly as he, she had no pretensions to valour, and her sex will excuse her.

The Captain, the priest, the officers, Valentine, Curio, even Fabian and Maria and Antonio, are the kind of characters E. M. Forster called flat. Not that we judge them the less real on that account, any more than a background seems, because less detailed, less real than the foreground. We know

Viola well; these others are acquaintances only, a society of potentials, alive enough without distracting. Occasionally what we thought background isn't. In *Julius Caesar*, Antony long seems a cameo part, like Cicero; Marullus and Flavius begin importantly, but aren't. This fact helps to create the illusion, within individual plays and across the canon, that any part of the background has its own foreground, which might become our foreground at any time. It suggests that all of the characters, even the flattest, have an unexpressed but expressible potency.

These minor characters not only enhance Viola's scale, or highlight certain of her features. She also responds appropriately to each. She gives Valentine prose and Orsino verse. She pounces upon Maria in a tone and idiom foreign to her conversations with Olivia. After the comic prose of the duel she honours Antonio with intense and thoughtful verse. Witty and at ease with Olivia, she has a marked reticence and seriousness with the Duke. Viola has like us all a social malleability, which occasionally stimulates from her reactions which elsewhere have no opportunity for expression. With Feste in 3.1, she accepts and even briefly contributes to his puns and sexual innuendoes; Aguecheek's French prompts French from her; Maria's and Toby's nautical metaphors make her speak sailor. These qualities, unsuspected until glimpsed, of course detail her character, but they do so not just by an arithmetic accumulation of one detail plus another, but suggestingly and as though geometrically. Viola knew French all along, but the fact had no occasion to surface. These and how many other attributes sleep in her awaiting expression, until a particular encounter and stimulus call them out. Viola need no more know French than her father need have had a mole upon his brow: like the Captain's birth "not three hours' travel from this very place," these are gratuitous particulars. They are not used but leak unconcernedly, an overflow of unfathomed possibility. Shakespeare establishes the uniformity of a voice by repetition, through habits of language, among them the tendency to sparse and elegant imagery, so that concentrations of imagery—particularly those that smack of jargon, or the colloquial—stand out emphatically from their context.

> I would be loath to cast away my speech, for besides that it is excellently well penned, I have taken great pains to con it. . . . I can say little more than I have studied, and that question's out of my part. . . . I am not that I play.

> MARIA. Will you hoist sail, sir? Here lies your way.
> VIOLA. No, good swabber, I am to hull here a little longer.

SIR TOBY. Will you encounter the house? My niece is very
    desirous you should enter, if your trade be to her.
VIOLA. I am bound to your niece, sir—I mean, she is the list
    of my voyage.

Her reactions to Maria and Toby may be mockery, may be the pretence of
hearty masculinity. It is in any case a language put on for the occasion, just
as her romantic diction is put on, when she plays ambassador. Likewise, in a
context of relatively unimaged speech, concentrations of intense and developing imagery convey climax and emphasis.

> Make me a willow cabin at your gate,
> And call upon my soul within the house;
> Write loyal cantons of contemned love,
> And sing them loud even in the dead of night;
> Halloo your name to the reverberate hills,
> And make the babbling gossip of the air
> Cry out "Olivia!" O, you should not rest
> Between the elements of air and earth,
> But you should pity me.

> A blank, my lord. She never told her love,
> But let concealment like a worm i'th' bud
> Feed on her damask cheek; she pin'd in thought,
> And with a green and yellow melancholy
> She sat like Patience on a monument,
> Smiling at grief. Was not this love indeed?
> We men may say more, swear more, but indeed
> Our shows are more than will: for still we prove
> Much in our vows, but little in our love.

Admittedly, our knowledge of Viola's secret alerts us to her feelings here,
but nothing immediately stimulates either release of poetry, and against
Viola's norm these two famous speeches do seem a release, which we
naturally and automatically interpret as the expression of emotions otherwise contained or suppressed. The second speech contradicts not only her
usual style, but also her usual pronounced reticence in Orsino's company. If
these images or those other masculine ones came unannounced, un-
prompted, not in clusters but here and there at random, they would be
wasted and unseen. They would only confuse not complicate the character.
Only the security of the norm alerts us to the significance of variation; as in
an experiment, Shakespeare varies only one factor at a time, keeping the

others constant. Moreover, in each instance he provides an immediately apprehensible stimulus or motive for the variation, whether it be Toby's ludicrous metaphor or Viola's secret, so that, again as in an experiment, by isolating the variable, Shakespeare illuminates the relation of cause to effect.

Thus to put side by side such moods and tones intimates layers and strata of personality, ever-present if only occasionally displayed. This trick of juxtaposition begins in Viola's first "parenthesis," where grief and a practical curiosity coexist. Moods or motifs once sounded may later be summoned and combined by the briefest allusion, as in

> I am all the daughters of my father's house,
> And all the brothers too—and yet I know not.
> Sir, shall I to this lady?

After the concealed longing of her talk with Orsino, the mention of her brother wakens another and unrelated longing, until the next line as abruptly returns us to the practical issue, Olivia, unmentioned now for almost forty lines. Again:

> VIOLA. I pity you.
> OLIVIA.   That's a degree of love.
> VIOLA. No, not a grize: for 'tis a vulgar proof
>   That very oft we pity enemies.

Viola's two versions of Olivia (as rival and fellow sufferer) here are yoked in all their unannealed disparity, as they were, less emphatically, when her sympathy for "poor Olivia" followed the success of her own curse. Moreover, this serious and simple "I pity you" itself stands out against Viola's lightheartedness in this scene, which began with Feste and, after this interruption, continues until she answers Olivia vow for vow.

If, as I. A. Richards said, metaphor is "the interanimation of contexts," or Dr Johnson's "unexpected copulation of ideas," such juxtapositions are metaphors: they force our imaginations to leap distinction and discover relation where there seems none. Metaphors implicate us; they make us act the text rather than receive it. Literalists dislike any fleshing out of the airy nothing of a dramatic fiction, but Shakespeare in constructing life advertises vacuums which demand filling, which imagination duly fills. This happens even in what [Levin L.] Schücking and [E. E.] Stoll would dismiss as "popular entertainment." In *City Lights*, Charlie Chaplin fights a boxing match to win money for a blind girl. Between rounds, he hallucinates that she is sponging his face. In the next and final round, he is losing badly and evidently exhausted, when suddenly and without explanation, in a burst of energy, he fights brilliantly and passionately, until finally he collapses. One cannot but notice the disjunction; one is *asked* to account for it. And the context provides an obvious explanation, that he suddenly remembers the purpose of the fight, and makes a last heroic effort. And, just as this technique can be found in "popular" drama, so it can be found in ancient drama, proving that there is nothing anachronistically "modern" about this notion of subtext. In Sophocles's *Antigone*, Creon's son Haemon never mentions his own love for Antigone, in the course of his long argument with his father (though it has been mentioned, earlier in the play, by Ismene); after that scene, the Chorus sings a stasimon to Ἔρως, "Love," a hymn which "has little to do with the main issue of the play." In the next scene Antigone, on her way to her death, laments her misfortunes, in particular regretting (three times: 813–16, 867, 876) that her early death robs her of the fulfilments of marriage. Yet, just as Haemon never mentions her, so she never mentions Haemon. Like Viola, Sophocles's lovers impress us partly by their emotional restraint. An audience cannot help but sense powerful emotions operating beneath the surface.

Chaplin, Sophocles and Shakespeare create a vacuum, and supply us with the means to fill it, so that, without ever imposing an explicit statement of motive, they make the unspoken chain of thought immediately apprehensible. Linking Viola's grief for Sebastian to her longing for Orsino suggests a predisposition and a pattern of mind, where we saw before only isolated, wholly independent reactions to circumstance. Her abrupt turn to the practical, by echoing the striking movement of her first scene, reinforces this pattern; further, it implies a repeated effort to suppress pain through action, an effort not entirely successful, since we see memories of Sebastian well up without warning, and since we understand her sublimated confessions to Orsino. Again, proximity of pity and enmity invites an explanation, for instance that her harshness means immediately to discourage Olivia's hopeless passion—just as, because we know Viola knows Olivia loves, we may interpret her witty deflections and interruptions earlier in this scene as a deliberate attempt to forestall unpleasantness. Viola's confession

> yet, a barful strife!
> Whoe'er I woo, myself would be his wife

likewise catalyses an alchemy of context, in that her reluctance to negotiate with Olivia—which we first take at face value, as characteristic self-doubt —seems now motivated in part or whole by private interests. The very forcing of the paradox into a couplet asks us how such feelings can accompany such actions. So by a metaphor of motive Shakespeare lures us into swamps of interpretation. In a Cleopatra or a Hamlet, these contradictions and contractions, huddled more frequently and violently together, continually tease us out of the text into exploration and connection. But the artistic principle (which we have seen in the small parentheses and digressions of unlinear dialogue, in the clash of styles, in the juxtaposition of opposed moods) is simple: an abrupt change of direction compels us to seek an explanation, on the evidence of what we already know about the character or the context, and that explanation in turn compels us to revise our picture of the character.

Shakespeare's Poetical Character in *Twelfth Night*

Geoffrey H. Hartman

Writing about Shakespeare promotes a sympathy with extremes. One such extreme is the impressionism of a critic like A. C. Bradley, when he tries to hold together, synoptically, Feste the fool and Shakespeare himself, both as actor and magical author. Bradley notes that the Fool in *Lear* has a song not dissimilar to the one that concludes *Twelfth Night* and leaves Feste at the finish line. "But that's all one, our play is done. . . ." After everything has been sorted out, and the proper pairings are arranged, verbal and structural rhythms converge to frame a sort of closure—though playing is never done, as the next and final verse suggests: "And we'll strive to please you every day." Bradley, having come to the end of an essay on Feste, extends *Twelfth Night* speculatively beyond the fool's song, and imagines Shakespeare leaving the theater:

> The same Shakespeare who perhaps had hummed the old song, half-ruefully and half-cheerfully, to its accordant air, as he walked home alone to his lodging, from the theatre or even from some noble's mansion; he who, looking down from an immeasurable height on the mind of the public and the noble, had yet to be their servant and jester, and to depend upon their favour; not wholly uncorrupted by this dependence, but yet superior to it and, also determined, like Feste, to lay by the sixpences it brought him, until at last he could say the word, "Our revels now are ended," and could break—was it a magician's staff or a Fool's bauble?

From *Shakespeare and the Question of Theory*, edited by Patricia Parker and Geoffrey H. Hartman. © 1985 by Geoffrey H. Hartman. Methuen, 1985.

The rhetoric of this has its own decorum. It aims to convey a general, unified impression of a myriad-minded artist. Shakespearean interpreters have a problem with *summing up*. Leaning on a repeated verse ("For the rain it raineth every day"), and more quietly on the iteration of the word "one" (*Lear*: "Poor Fool and knave, I have one part in my heart / That's sorry yet for thee"; *Feste*: "I was one, sir, in this interlude; one Sir Topas, sir, but that's all one"), Bradley integrates Shakespeare by the deft pathos of an imaginary portrait. Today's ideological critics would probably purge this portrait of everything but Shakespeare's representation of power-relations and hierarchy. Such critics might note that the portrait's final question serves only to emphasize the artist's marginality, his loneliness or apartness, as if by a secret law of fate being an artist excluded Shakespeare from social power in the very world he addresses.

The relation of "character" in the world (domestic or political) to "poetical character" (the imaginary relations to that same world which make up our image of a particular artist) is always elusive. Especially so in the case of Shakespeare, of whose life we know so little. A myth evolves, given classic expression by Keats, that the mystery or obscurity enveloping Shakespeare's life is due to the fact that a great poet has no "identity," that he is "everything and nothing"—as Bradley's evocation also suggests. John Middleton Murry's book on Shakespeare begins with a chapter entitled "Everything and Nothing" in which Murry explores his reluctant conclusion that "In the end there is nothing to do but to surrender to Shakespeare." "The moment comes in our experience of Shakespeare when we are dimly conscious of a choice to be made: either we must turn away (whether by leaving him in silence, or by substituting for his reality some comfortable intellectual fiction of our own), or we must suffer ourselves to be drawn into the vortex."

The focus moves, in short, to the character of the critic, determined by this choice. Can *we* abide Shakespeare's question? Does the critic have a "character" of his own, or is he simply a bundle of responses accommodated to a special institution or audience: university students and dons, or other drama buffs, or the general public? Unlike Eliot, say, or Tolstoy, Murry has no body of creative writing to back up the importance of his interpretive engagements. There is, nevertheless, a sense that the critic's identity is formed by his selfless encounters with artists of Shakespeare's stature.

The "vortex" that threatens readers, according to Murry, includes the fact that Shakespeare delights as much in Iago as Imogen (Keats's words); and to shuffle off our ordinary conceptions of character—in Murry's phrase, the "mortal coil of moral judgment"—is both painful and necessary. Always, Murry claims, "when Shakespeare has been allowed to make *his* impression, we find the critic groping after the paradox of the poetical character itself as described by Keats." In an earlier essay, closer to Bradley's era, Murry had already put the problem of Shakespeare criticism in terms that showed how aware he was of reactions to the "vortex." He rejects the " 'idea'-bacillus" that reduces Shakespeare to universal themes or the creation of character-types, yet he refuses to relinquish his rigorous quest for "the center of comprehension from which he [Shakespeare] worked." Programmatic as it is, Murry's statement of 1920 remains relevant:

> Let us away then with "logic" and away with "ideas" from the art of literary criticism; but not, in a foolish and impercipient reaction, to revive the impressionistic criticism which has sapped the English brain for a generation past. The art of criticism is rigorous; impressions are merely its raw material; the life-blood of its activity is in the process of ordonnance of aesthetic impressions.

The rejection of impressionism leads, if we think of Eliot, and of Murry himself, simply to a more rigorous formulation of the paradox of the impersonal artist. For Murry it meant comparing Christian and post-Shakespearean (especially Romantic) ways of annihilating selfhood. Blake becomes even more crucial for such a formulation than Keats. G. W. Knight also joins this quest. Other rigorous escape routes, that lead through impressionism beyond it, make Shakespeare's language the main character of his plays, the everything and nothing. Empson's colloquial fracturing of Shakespeare's text, from *Seven Types* through *Complex Words*, as well as Leavis's emphasis on the "heuristico-creative quality of the diction" avoid, on the whole, totalizing structures. Rigor consists in having the local reading undo an established symmetry.

Another form of rigor, historical scholarship, can be outrageously speculative. (The trend was always there in the work of editors who unscrambled perplexing expressions or normalized daring ones.) One might escape the Shakespearean vortex by discovering a firm historical emplacement for the plays, by clarifying their occasion as well as the characters in them. The work of referring the plays back to sources mysteriously transformed by Shakespeare (minor Italian novellas, or poetics derived from Donatus and Terence, such as the "forward progress of the turmoils") gives way to an ambitious reconstruction of a particular, sponsoring event. The quest for the identity of W. H. or the Dark Lady or the exact festive occasion of *Twelfth Night* exerts a prosecutory charm that attests to the presence of character in the critic-investigator (that stubborn, scholarly sleuth) as well as in Shakespeare the historical personage. Consider what the ingenious Leslie Hotson does with the "jest nominal," or play on names. It is as intriguing as anything ventured by newfangled intertextualists.

Hotson claims in *The First Night of Twelfth Night* that the figure of Malvolio is a daring take-off of a high official in Elizabeth's court: Sir William Knollys, Earl of Banbury and Controller of her Majesty's household. This aging dignitary, we are told, had become infatuated with a young Maid of Honor at Court, Mall (Mary) Fitton. In the "allowed fooling" of Twelfth Night festivities, "old Beard Knollys," suggests Hotson, "is slaughtered in gross and detail." Here is his description of how it was done

> while exposing both the Controller's *ill-will*—towards hilarity and misrule—and his *amorousness* in the name *Mala-voglia* (Ill Will *or* Evil concupiscence) Shakespeare also deftly fetches up Knollys' ridiculous love-chase of Mistress Mall by a sly modulation of *Mala-Voglia* into "*Mal*"-*voglio*—which means "I want Mall," "I wish for Mall," "I will have Mall." It is a masterpiece of mockery heightened by merciless repetition, with the players ringing the changes of expression on "*Mal*"-*voglio* . . . it will bring down the house.

The play becomes a *roman à clef*, and so delivers us from a verbal vertigo it exposes. Shakespeare's improvisational genius, moreover, his extreme wit and opportunism, may recall the methodical *bricolage* by which earlier mythmakers, according to Lévi-Strauss, sustained their tale. Here it explicitly pleases or shames the ears of a court-centered audience. Yet this shaming or delighting is not necessarily in the service of good sense or the status quo, for it can subvert as well as mock and purge. The one thing it does, as in the case of the Controller, is to acknowledge the law of gender—of generation and succession—which, as Erasmus saw, compels us to play the fool. Such allowed slander, whether or not reinforced by Elizabethan festivities, by periods of compulsory license, also penetrates Shakespearean tragedy:

> Even he, the father of gods and king of men, who shakes all heaven by a nod, is obliged to lay aside his three-pronged thunder and that Titanic aspect by which, when he pleases, he scares all the

gods, and assume another character in the slavish manner of an actor, if he wishes to do what he never refrains from doing, that is to say, to beget children. . . . He will certainly lay by his gravity, smooth his brow, renounce his rock-bound principles, and for a few minutes toy and talk nonsense. . . . Venus herself would not deny that without the addition of my presence her strength would be enfeebled and ineffectual. So it is that from this brisk and silly little game of mine come forth the haughty philosophers.

II

Generation and Succession are so fundamental to almost all classes and types of humanity that to reduce them to their verbal effects might seem trivializing. Yet, as Erasmus's Folly hints, the very category of the trivial is overturned by these forces. The "striving to please every day," which is the fate of the player, is equally that of lover and courtier. It quickens even as it exhausts our wit. It points to a relentless need for devices—words, stratagems. More is required than a "tiny little wit" to sustain what every day demands.

There exist eloquent characterizations of Shakespeare's understanding of the common nature of mankind. As Bakhtin remarks of another great writer, Rabelais, there are crownings and uncrownings at every level. No one is exempt, at any time, from that rise and fall, whether it is brought on by actual political events or social and sexual rivalry, or internalized pressures leading to self-destructive illusions and acts. The vicissitudes of Folly and Fortuna go hand in hand. Yet no conclusions are drawn; and it does not matter what class of person is involved—a Falstaff, a Harry, a King Henry; a clown, a count, a lady; a usurper, a porter. What happens happens across the board, and can therefore settle expressively in a language with a character of its own—apart from the decorum that fits it to the character of the person represented. The pun or quibble, Shakespeare's "fatal Cleopatra," is a quaint and powerful sign of that deceiving variety of life. Hazlitt, following Charles Lamb, remarks that Elizabethan "distinctions of dress, the badges of different professions, the very signs of the shops" were a sort of visible language for the imagination. "The surface of society was embossed with hieroglyphs." Yet the showiest and most self-betraying thing in Shakespeare is the flow of language itself, which carries traces of an eruption from some incandescent and molten core, even when hard as basalt, that is, patently rhetorical.

Structurally too, the repetitions by which we discover an intent—a purposiveness—do not resolve themselves into a unity, a "one" free of sexual, hierarchical or personal differentiation. Feste's "one" is an Empsonian complex word, which seeks to distract us, by its very iteration, into a sense of closure. Yet there is never an objective correlative that sops up the action or organizes all the excrescent motives and verbal implications. Feste's phrase is found, for example, in the mouth of another clown figure, Fluellen, in a scene one could characterize as "Porn at Monmouth" (*Henry V*, 4.7). The scene, through the solecisms and mispronunciations of Fluellen, his butchery of English, makes us aware of what is involved in the larger world of combat, to which he is marginal. The catachresis of "Kill the Poyes and the luggage!" expresses the cut-throat speed with which matters are moving toward indiscriminate slaughter. An end penetrates the middle of the drama; the grimace (if only linguistic) of death begins to show through.

Yet even here, as the action hits a dangerous juncture, as decisions become hasty and bloody, this verbally excessive interlude slows things down to a moment of humorous discrimination. Fluellen draws a comparison between Harry of Monmouth and "Alexander the Pig" of Macedon (*Henry V*, 4.7). That "big" should issue as "pig" is a fertile and leveling pun, which the macabre turn of this near-graveyard scene could have exploited even more; but the uncrowning of Alexander in Fluellen's mouth leads to a series of images (mouth, fingers, figures) that suggest a "body" less mortal than its parts. Harry's transformation into King Henry, and Fluellen's comparison in his favor—that Harry's bloodthirsty anger is more justified than Alexander's—appear like a jesting in the throat of death, a vain distinction already undone by the battlefield context that levels all things, as by an earthy vernacular, or quasi-vernacular, that can slander all things in perfect good humor.

It seems impossible, then, to describe the poetical character of Shakespeare without raising certain questions. One concerns the character of the critic (choices to be made in reading so strong and productive a writer); another what happens to language as it nurtures a vernacular ideal that still dominates English literature. A third, related question is whether what that language does to character and to us can be summed up or unified by methodical inquiry. Does an "intellectual tradition" exist, as Richards thought, to guide us in reading that plentiful "Elizabethan" mixture? "The hierarchy of these modes is elaborate and variable," he writes about sixteenth- and seventeenth-century literature. To "read aright," Richards continues, "we need to shift with an at present indescribable adroitness and celerity from one mode to another."

By "modes" Richards means different types of indirect statement, which he also characterizes as "metaphorical, allegorical, symbolical," yet does not define further. In some way they are all nonliteral; at least not directly literal. Like Coleridge, whom he quotes, Richards is impressed by the role that "wit" plays in Shakespeare's time, although he does not discuss the complicit or antagonistic and always showy relation between wit and will. He simply accepts Coleridge's thesis on wit and Shakespeare's time

> when the English Court was still foster-mother of the State and the Muses; and when, in consequence, the courtiers and men of rank and fashion affected a display of wit, point, and sententious observation, that would be deemed intolerable at present—but in which a hundred years of controversy, involving every great political, and every dear domestic interest, had trained all but the lowest classes to participate. Add to this the very style of the sermons of the time, and the eagerness of the Protestants to distinguish themselves by long and frequent preaching, and it will be found that, from the reign of Henry VIII to the abdication of James II, no country ever received such a national education as England.

Yet Coleridge's notion of "national education" may be too idealistic—Arnoldian before the letter. It downplays the subverting character of Shakespeare's wit, one that is not put so easily in the service of the nation-state and its movement toward a common language. The "prosperity of a pun," as M. M. Mahood calls it, in what is still the most sensitive exploration of the subject, offended rather than pleased most refiners of English up to modern times. "Prosperity" may itself covertly play on "propriety," which is precisely what a pun questions. The speed and stenography, in any case, of Shakespeare's wordplay in the comic scenes undoes the hegemony of any single order of discourse, and compels us to realize the radically social and mobile nature of the language exchange. And, unlike the novel (which allows Bakhtin his most persuasive theorizing), these scenes display less a narrative or a pseudonarrative than oral graffiti. Verbally Shakespeare is a graffiti artist, using bold, often licentious strokes, that make sense because of the living context of stereotypes, the *commedia dell'arte*, and other vernacular or popular traditions.

Is it possible, then, to see Shakespeare *sub specie unitatis*, as the younger Murry thought? "There never has been and never will be a human mind which can resist such an inquiry if it is pursued with sufficient perseverance and understanding." Yet in this very sentence "human mind" is fleetingly equivocal: does it refer only to the object of inquiry, Shakespeare's mind, or also to the interpreter's intellect, tempted by the riddle of Shakespeare? The later Murry too does not give up; but now the unity, the "all that's one," is frightening as well, and associated with *omnia abeunt in mysterium:* all things exit into mystery.

It seems to me there is no mystery, no *Abgrund*, except language itself, whose revelatory revels are being staged, as if character were a function of language, rather than vice versa. More precisely, as if the locus of the dramatic action were the effect of language on character. *Twelfth Night* will allow us to examine how this language test is applied. If we admire, however ambivalently, the way Iago works on Othello by "damnable iteration" (cf. *Falstaff:* "O, thou hast damnable iteration, and art indeed able to corrupt a saint," *Henry IV, Part 1,* 1.2.90), or the way Falstaff shamelessly converts abuse into flattery, we are already caught up in a rhetoric whose subversive motility, moment to moment, can bless or curse, praise or blame, corrupt words or (like Aristotle's eulogist) substitute collateral terms that "lean toward the best." It is this instant possibility of moving either way, or simultaneously both ways, which defines the Shakespearean dramatic and poetical character. In *Twelfth Night*, with Feste a self-pronounced "corrupter of words" (3.1.37), and Malvolio's censorious presence, the verbal action challenges all parties to find "comic remedies," or to extract sweets from weeds and poisons.

III

"Excellent," says Sir Toby Belch, "I smell a device." "I have't in my nose too," Sir Andrew Aguecheek echoes him (2.3.162). Toby is referring to the plan concocted by Maria, Olivia's maid, of how to get even with the strutting and carping Malvolio, steward of the household. The device is a letter to be written by Maria in her lady's hand, which will entice Malvolio into believing Olivia is consumed with a secret passion for him, his yellow stockings, cross-garters and smile. The device (not the only one in the play—Bertrand Evans has counted seven persons who are active practisers operating six devices) succeeds; and Malvolio, smiling hard, and wearing the colors he thinks are the sign commanded by his lady, but which she happens to detest, is taken for mad and put away.

The very words "I smell a device" contain a device. Toby, mostly drunk, knows how to choose his metaphors; and Andrew, not much of a wit ("I am a great eater of beef, and I believe that does harm to my wit"), merely echoes him, which makes the metaphor more literal and so more absurd. A device is also a figure, or flower of speech; both meanings may be present here, since the content of the device is literary, that is, a deceivingly flowery letter. Flowers smell, good or bad as the occasion may be. "Lillies that fester smell far worse than weeds" (Sonnet 94). Sometimes figures or metaphors fly by so thick and fast that we all are as perplexed as Sir Andrew:

ANDREW. Bless you, fair shrew.

MARIA. And you too, sir.

TOBY. Accost, Sir Andrew, accost. . . .

ANDREW. Good Mistress Accost, I desire better acquaintance.

MARIA. My name is Mary, sir.

ANDREW. Good Mistress Mary Accost—

TOBY. You mistake, knight. "Accost" is front her, board her, woo her, assail her.

ANDREW. By my troth, I would not undertake her in this company. Is that the meaning of "accost"?

MARIA. Fare you well, gentlemen.

TOBY. And thou let part so, Sir Andrew, would thou might'st never draw sword again!

ANDREW. And you part so, mistress, I would I might never draw sword again. Fair lady, do you think you have fools in hand?

MARIA. Sir, I have not you by th' hand.

ANDREW. Marry, but you shall have, and here's my hand.

MARIA. Now, sir, thought is free. I pray you bring your hand to th' buttery bar and let it drink.

ANDREW. Wherefore, sweetheart? What's your metaphor?

MARIA. It's dry, sir.

(1.3.46–72)

Awkward Andrew starts with a mild oxymoron and compounds the error of his address to Mary by a further innocent mistake—the transposition of a common verb into a proper noun, which not only unsettles parts of speech but creates a parallel euphemism to "fair shrew" through the idea of "good Accost." The entire scene is constructed out of such pleasant errors—failed connections or directions that hint at larger, decisive acts (accosting, undertaking, marrying). At line 62 the verbal plot becomes even more intricate, as Andrew strives to "address" Mary a second time. "Marry" (66) is an oath, a corruption of the Virgin's name; but here, in addition to echoing "Mary," it may be the common verb, as Andrew tries to be witty or gallant by saying in a slurred way (hey, I too can fling metaphors around!), "If you marry you'll have me by the hand, and here it is." (He forgets that that would make him a fool, like all married men.) Maria bests him, though, suggesting a freer kind of handling, with a new metaphor that—I think—may be licentious. What is that "buttery bar"? Probably, in function, a bar as today, for serving drinks; but could it be her breasts or . . . butt? That same "bar," by a further twist or trope, echoes in Maria's "marry, now I let go your hand, I am barren" (77). No wonder Andrew, out of his range, stutters, "Wherefore, sweetheart? What's your metaphor?"

Somewhere there is always a device, or a "hand" that could fool just about anyone. Nobody is spared, nobody escapes witting. Yet it remains harmless because all, except Malvolio, play along. There is rhetoric and repartee, puns and paranomasia, metaphor upon metaphor, as if these characters were signifying monkeys: the play expects every person to pass the test of wit, to stand at that bar of language. Yet "wherefore?" we ask, like simple Andrew.

That question returns us to the poetical character. It "is not itself," Keats wrote, "it has no self—it is every thing and nothing—It has no character." He says other things, too, which make it clear he is thinking mainly of Shakespeare. "It lives in gusto, be it foul or fair, high or low, rich or poor, mean or elevated—It has as much delight in conceiving an Iago as an Imogen. What shocks the virtuous philosopher [a Malvolio in this respect] delights the chameleon Poet. It does no harm from its relish of the dark side of things any more than for its taste for the bright one; because they both end in speculation" (letter to Richard Woodhouse, October 27, 1818).

Much depends on that word "speculation" in Keats; a "widening speculation," he also writes, eases the burden of life's mystery, takes away the heat and fever (letter to J. H. Reynolds, May 3, 1818). You have to have something to speculate with or on; some luxury, like a delicious voice, whose first impact you remember. Speculation is making the thing count again, as with money, yet *without fearing its loss*. The Shakespearean language of wit is like that. Though penetrated by knowledge of loss, aware that the most loved or fancied thing can fall "into abatement and low price, / Even in a minute!" (1.1.13–14), it still spends itself in an incredibly generous manner, as if the treasury of words were always full. However strange it may seem, while everything in this play is, emotionally, up or down—each twin, for example, thinks the other dead; Olivia, in constant mourning and rejecting Orsino, is smitten by Viola / Cesario in the space of one interview—while everything vacillates, the language itself coins its metaphors and fertile exchanges beyond any calculus of loss and gain. When I hear the word "fool" repeated so many times, I also hear the word "full" emptied out or into it; so "Marry" and "Mary" and "madam" ("maddame") and "madman" collapse distinctions of character (personality) in favor of some prodigious receptacle that "receiveth as the sea" (1.1.11). No wonder modern critics have felt a Dionysian drift in the play, a doubling and effacing of persons as well as a riot of metaphors working against distinctions, until, to quote the ballad at the end, "that's all one."

IV

I think, therefore I am. What does one do about "I act" or "I write"? What identity for that "I"? For the poet who shows himself in the inventive wit of all these personae? *Twelfth Night* gives an extraordinary amount of theatrical time to Sir Toby Belch and Sir Andrew Aguecheek, and to clowning generally. These scenes threaten to erupt into the main plot, which is absurd enough, where love is sudden and gratuitous, as in Orsino's infatuation for Olivia (two O's) or Viola's for Orsino, or Olivia's for Cesario. Everything goes o–a in this play, as if a character's destiny depended on voweling. "M.O.A.I. doth sway my life" (2.5.109). Whose *hand* directs this comic tumult of mistaken identities, disguises, devices, and names, that even when they are not Rabelaisian or musical scrabble (Olivia: Viola) or transparent like Malvolio (the evil eye, or evil wish) are silly attempts at self-assertion? So it doesn't really help when Sebastian in 2.1.14–18 identifies himself. "You must know of me then, Antonio, my name is Sebastian, which I called Roderigo; my father was that Sebastian of Messaline whom I know you have heard of." We have two Sebastians, and one Sebastian is Roderigo. In addition, as we know by this point in the drama, Sebastian and Viola (that is, Cesario) are identical twins, born in the same hour, both saved from the "breach" a second time when they escape shipwreck and find themselves in a land with the suggestive name of Illyria—compounded, to the sensitive ear, out of Ill and liar/lyre. So also Viola enters the play punning, or off-rhyming. "And what should I do in Illyria? / My brother he is in Elysium" (1.2.3–4).

The question, then, relates to identity and destiny, or who has what in hand; it is also related to the question of questioning itself, that kind of speech-act, so close to trial and testing, and the legalese or academic lingo in a play perhaps performed at an inn-of-court. In late medieval times, from the twelfth century on, there was a shift in "pedagogical technique (and

corresponding literary forms) from the *lectio* to the *disputatio* and *questio* . . .
from primary concern for the exegesis of authoritative texts and the laying
of doctrinal foundations toward the resolution of particular (and sometimes
minor) difficulties and even the questioning of matters no longer seriously
doubted, for the sake of exploring the implications of a doctrine, revealing
the limits of necessity and contingency, or demonstrating one's dialectical
skills." Another authority writes that "Even the points accepted by everybody and set forth in the most certain of terms were brought under scrutiny
and subjected, by deliberate artifice, to the now usual processes of research.
In brief, they were, literally speaking, 'called into question,' no longer
because there was any real doubt about their truth, but because a deeper
understanding of them was sought after." From contemporary reports of
the "Acts" at Oxford when Elizabeth visited, we know that these questions
and *quodlibets* maintained themselves at least ceremonially. Is *Twelfth Night*'s
subtitle, "What You Will," a jocular translation of *quodlibet*? What significance may there be in the fact that in 1.3.86–96 Toby passes from "No
question" to "*Pourquoi*" to "Past question?" My own question is: *Pourquoi*
these "kikshawses" ("quelques choses")? Wherefore, Shakespeare? What's
your metaphor for?

Testing and questing seem connected immemorially: it is hard to think
of the one without the other, especially in the realm of "Acts" which assert
authority or identity by playful display. Even the Academy participates that
much in the realm of romance. But my comments are meant to lead somewhat deeper into a drama that relishes the night-side of things with such
good humor. If there are low-class mistakes, as when Andrew thinks
Toby's "Accost" refers to Mary's name, there are also the high-class mistakes, Orsino's love, principally, that starts the play with a fine call for
music in verses intimating that nothing can fill desire, fancy, love. Its appetite is like the sea, so capacious, so swallowing and changeable. "If music
be the food of love, play on." *Play on* is what we do, as "Misprision in the
highest degree" (1.5.53) extends itself. Everything changes place or is mistaken, so that Orsino believes himself in love with Olivia but settles "dex-
teriously," as the Clown might say, for Viola; while poor Malvolio is taken
for mad and confined in a place as gloomy as his temperament. We tumble
through the doubling, reversing, mistaking, clowning, even cloning; we
never get away from the tumult of the words themselves, from the "gratillity" (another clown-word, that is, gratuitousness or greed for tips, tipsi-
ness) of Feste's "gracious fooling," as when Andrew, probably tipsy himself, and stupidly good at mixing metaphors, mentions some of the clown's

other coinages: "Pigrogromitus" and the "Vapians passing the equinoctial of Queubus" (2.3.23–24).

It is not that these funny, made-up words don't make sense: they make a kind of instant sense, as Shakespeare always does. Yet a sense that can't be proved, that remains to be guessed at and demands something from us. Does "equinoctial" hint at solstice or equinox festivals, if *Twelfth Night* was performed on the day the title suggests; is "Queubus" mock Latin for the tail or male, or a corruption of "quibus," "a word of frequent occurrence in legal documents and so associated with verbal niceties or subtle distinctions" (C. T. Onions)? Did the audience know it was slang for fool in Dutch ("Kwibus")?

The text requires a certain tolerance or liberality of interpretation: yellow cross-garters in the realm of construing, "motley in the brain" (1.5.55). To quote Andrew—and it should be inscribed on the doors of all literature departments: "I would I had bestowed that time in the tongues that I have in fencing, dancing, and bear-baiting. O, had I but followed the arts!" (1.3.90–93).

There exists a modern version of another "antic" song about the twelve days of Christmas (cf. 2.3.85). If Twelfth Night, the climax of Christmastide rejoicing, asks that we fill up the daystar's ebb, then the emphasis falls on giving, on true-love giving. Twelfth Night, formally the feast of Epiphany, is when divinity appeared, when Christ was manifested to the Gentiles (the Magi or three kings). Presence rather than absence is the theme. *Twelfth Night* is not a religious play, and yet its "gracious fooling" may be full of grace. The great O of Shakespeare's stage draws into it the gift of tongues; and in addition to the legal or academic metaphors, the food and sexual metaphors, and other heterogeneous language strains, occasionally a religious pathos, impatient of all these indirections, maskings, devices, makes itself heard. "Wherefore are these things hid? Wherefore have these gifts a curtain before 'em?" (1.3.122–23) To the question, what filling (fulfilling) is in this fooling, the best reply might be that, in literature, everything aspires to the condition of language, to the gift of tongues; that the spirit—wanton as it may be—of language overrides such questions, including those of character and identity.

Does Orsino, the Duke, have an identity, or is he not a plaything of fancy; and is love not represented by him as both arbitrary in what it fixes on and as "full of shapes" and "fantastical" as the entire play? These people seem in love with words rather than with each other. More exactly, the embassy of words and the play of rhetoric are essential tests for both lover and object of love. When Curio tries to distract the Duke from his musical and effete reflections by "Will you go hunt, my lord?" (1.1.16), Orsino answers, startled, "What, Curio?" meaning "What d'you say?" which is misunderstood when Curio replies, "The hart," after which the Duke can't restrain himself from an old quibble equating hart, the animal, and heart, the seat of love:

> Why, so I do [hunt], the noblest that I have.
> O, when mine eyes did see Olivia first,
> Methought she purg'd the air of pestilence;
> That instant was I turn'd into a hart,
> And my desires, like fell and cruel hounds,
> E'er since pursue me.
>
> (1.1.18–23)

The hunter becomes the hunted; but it is also suggested (though we may not be convinced) that the Duke finds a heart in himself—a sensitivity where previously there was nothing but a sense of privilege.

We see how thorough this full fooling is. In Shakespeare the poetry—the prose too—is larger than the characters, enlarging them but also making their identities or egos devices in an overwhelming revel. The revels of language are never ended. This does not mean that language is discontinuous with the search for identity or a "heart." Orsino's first speech already introduces the gracious theme of giving and receiving, of feeding, surfeiting, dying, reviving, playing on. Love and music are identified through the metaphor of the "dying fall" (1.1.4), also alluding, possibly, to the end of the year; and, ironically enough, the Duke's moody speech suggests *a desire to get beyond desire*—to have done with such perturbations, with wooing and risking rejection, and trying to win through by gifts and maneuvers. "Give me excess of it, that, surfeiting, / The appetite [for love, not just for music] may sicken, and so die" (1.1.2–3). At the very end of the play, with the Clown's final song, this melancholy desire to be beyond desire returns in the refrain "The rain it raineth every day," and the internal chiming of "that's all one, our play is done." Even in this generous and least cynical of Shakespeare's comedies, love is an appetite that wants to be routinized or exhausted, and so borders on tragic sentiments.

In drama, giving and receiving take the form of dialogic repartee. Shakespeare makes of dialogue a charged occasion, two masked affections testing each other, always on guard. Usually, then, there is a healthy fear or respect for the other; or there is a subversive sense that what goes on in human relations is not dialogue at all but seduction and domination. To

have real giving and receiving—in terms of speech and understanding—
may be so strenuous that the mind seeks other ways to achieve a sim-
ulacrum of harmony: maybe an "equinoctial of Queubus" brings us into
equilibrium, or maybe festivals, like Christmas, when there is at-one-ment,
through licensed license, through the principle of "what you will," of freely
doing or not doing. (Twelve, after all, is the sign of the temporal clock
turning over into One.) But the turn is felt primarily at the level of "gracious fooling" in this Christmas play. Hazlitt goes so far as to say "It is
perhaps too good-natured for comedy. It has little satire and no spleen."
And he continues with an even more significant remark, which I now want
to explore: "In a word, the best turn is given to everything, instead of the
worst."

V

The poetical genius of Shakespeare is inseparable from an ability to
trope anything and turn dialogue, like a fluctuating battle, to the worst or
best surmise. I see the dramatic and linguistic action of *Twelfth Night* as a
turning away of the evil eye. It averts a malevolent interpretation of life,
basically Malvolio's. Though Malvolio is unjustly—by a mere "device"—
put into a dark place, this too is for the good, for he must learn how to
plead. That is, by a quasilegal, heartfelt rhetoric, he must now turn the
evidence, from bad to good. In 4.2.12ff. a masquerade is acted out which
not only compels us to sympathize with Malvolio, making him a figure of
pathos, but which repeats, as a play within the play, the action of the whole.
Malvolio is gulled once more, baited like a bear—the sport he objected to.
Yet the spirit of this comedy is not that of revenge, malice or ritual expulsion. All these motives may participate, yet what rouses our pity and fear is
the way language enters and preordains the outcome. Shakespeare brings
out the schizoid nature of discourse by juxtaposing soft or good words,
ordinary euphemisms ("Jove bless thee, Master Parson," "*Bonos dies*, Sir
Toby," "Peace in this prison") with abusive imprecations ("Out, hyper-
bolical fiend," "Fie, thou dishonest Satan," "Madman, thou errest"). Malvolio is subjected to a ridiculous legal or religious quizzing: a "trial" by
"constant question." As in so many infamous state proceedings, he can get
nowhere. He has to cast himself, against his temperament, on the mercy of
the clown he condemned, though never actually harmed: "Fool, I say,"
"Good fool, as ever thou wilt deserve well at my hand," "Ay, good fool,"
"Fool, fool, fool, I say!" "Good fool, help me to some light and some
paper: I tell thee I am as well in my wits as any man in Illyria" ("*Feste:*

"Well-a-day that you were, sir"), "By this hand, I am! Good fool, some ink, paper, and light."

Every word suddenly receives its full value. A man's life or freedom depends on it. It is not quibbled away. Yet words remain words; they have to be received; the imploration is all. "By this hand" is more than a tender of good faith, the visible sign of imploration. It is the handwriting that could save Malvolio, as that other "hand," Maria's letter-device, fooled and trapped him. Ink, paper, and light, as for Shakespeare himself perhaps, are the necessities. They must dispel or counter-fool whatever plot has been, is being, woven.

The spectator sits safely, like a judge, on the bench; yet the reversal which obliges Malvolio to plead with the fool reminds us what it means to be dependent on what we say and how (generously or meanly) it is received. To please every day, like a courtier, lover or actor, leads us into improvisations beyond the ordinary scope of wit. It puts us all in the fool's place. It is everyone, not Feste alone, who is involved, when after a sally of nonsense Maria challenges him with "Make that good" (1.5.7). That is, give it meaning, in a world where "hanging" and "colours" (collars, cholers, flags, figures of speech, 1.5.1–6) are realities. But also, to return to Hazlitt's insight, give what you've said the best turn, justify the metaphor at whatever bar (legal) or buttery (the milk of mercy) is the least "dry" (1.3.72). "The rain it raineth every day."

Bakhtin's view, inspired by the development of literary vernaculars in the Renaissance, that each national language is composed of many kinds of discourse, dialogic even when not formally so, and polyphonic in effect, can be extended to the question of Shakespeare's poetical character. There is no one heart or one will ("Will"). Andrew's querulous "What's your metaphor?" or Maria's testing "Make it good" or the Clown's patter (" 'That that is, is'; so I, being Master Parson, am Master Parson; for what is 'that' but 'that'? and 'is' but 'is'?" [4.2.15–17]) impinge also on the spectator /reader. Yet in this world of figures, catches, errors, reversals, songs, devices, plays within plays, where motley distinguishes more than the jester, and even Malvolio is gulled into a species of it, moments arise that suggest a more than formal resolution—more than the fatigue or resignation of "that's all one" or the proverbial "all's well that ends well." So when Viola, as the Duke's go-between, asks Olivia, "Good madam, let me see your face" (where the "good," as in all such appeals, is more than an adjective, approaching the status of an absolute construction: "Good, madam," similar in force to Maria's "Make it good"), there is the hint of a possible revelatory moment, of clarification. The challenge, moreover, is met by a facing up to it. Yet the metaphor of expositing a text, which had preceded, is continued, so that we remain in the text even when we are out of it.

> OLIVIA. Now, sir, what is your text?
> VIOLA. Most sweet lady—
> OLIVIA. A comfortable doctrine, and much may be said of it.
> Where lies your text?
> VIOLA. In Orsino's bosom.
> OLIVIA. In his bosom? In what chapter of his bosom?
> VIOLA. To answer by the method, in the first of his heart.
> OLIVIA. O, I have read it: it is heresy. Have you no more to
> say?
> VIOLA. Good madam, let me see your face.
> OLIVIA. Have you any commission from your lord to negotiate
> with my face? You are now out of your text: but we will
> draw the curtain and show you the picture. [*Unveiling*]
> Look you, sir, such a one I was this present. Is't not well
> done?
> VIOLA. Excellently done, if God did all.

(1.5.223–39)

I was, not I am; by pretending she is a painting, just unveiled, the original I is no longer there, or only as this picture which points to a present in the way names or texts point to a meaning. The text, however, keeps turning. There is no "present": no absolute gift, or moment of pure being. Yet a sense of epiphany, however fleeting, is felt; a sense of mortality too and of artifice, as the text is sustained by the force of Olivia's wit. "Is't not well done?" Olivia, like Feste, must "make it good." The mocking elaboration of her own metaphor allows speech rather than embarrassed or astonished silence at this point. The play (including Olivia's "interlude") continues. There is always more to say.

Chronology

1564	William Shakespeare born at Stratford-on-Avon to John Shakespeare, a butcher, and Mary Arden. He is baptized on April 26.
1582	Marries Anne Hathaway in November.
1583	Daughter Susanna born, baptized on May 26.
1585	Twins Hamnet and Judith born, baptized on February 2.
1588–90	Sometime during these years, Shakespeare goes to London, without family. First plays performed in London.
1590–92	*The Comedy of Errors*, the three parts of *Henry VI*.
1593–94	Publication of *Venus and Adonis* and *The Rape of Lucrece*, both dedicated to the Earl of Southampton. Shakespeare becomes a sharer in the Lord Chamberlain's company of actors. *The Taming of the Shrew*, *The Two Gentlemen of Verona*, *Richard III*.
1595–97	*Romeo and Juliet*, *Richard II*, *King John*, *A Midsummer Night's Dream*, *Love's Labor's Lost*.
1596	Son Hamnet dies. Grant of arms to father.
1597	*The Merchant of Venice*, *Henry IV*, *Part 1*. Purchases New Place in Stratford.
1598–1600	*Henry IV*, *Part 2*, *As You Like It*, *Much Ado About Nothing*, *Twelfth Night*, *The Merry Wives of Windsor*, *Henry V*, and *Julius Caesar*. Moves his company to the new Globe Theatre.
1601	*Hamlet*. Shakespeare's father dies, buried on September 8.
1603	Death of Queen Elizabeth; James VI of Scotland becomes James I of England; Shakespeare's company becomes the King's Men.
1603–4	*All's Well That Ends Well*, *Measure for Measure*, *Othello*.
1605–6	*King Lear*, *Macbeth*.

147

1607	Marriage of daughter Susanna on June 5.
1607–8	*Timon of Athens, Antony and Cleopatra, Pericles.*
1608	Shakespeare's mother dies, buried on September 9.
1609	*Cymbeline*, publication of sonnets. Shakespeare's company purchases Blackfriars Theatre.
1610–11	*The Winter's Tale, The Tempest.* Shakespeare retires to Stratford.
1616	Marriage of daughter Judith on February 10. William Shakespeare dies at Stratford on April 23.
1623	Publication of the Folio edition of Shakespeare's plays.

Contributors

Harold Bloom, Sterling Professor of the Humanities at Yale University, is the author of *The Anxiety of Influence, Poetry and Repression*, and many other volumes of literary criticism. His forthcoming study, *Freud: Transference and Authority*, attempts a full-scale reading of all of Freud's major writings. A MacArthur Prize Fellow, he is general editor of five series of literary criticism published by Chelsea House. During 1987 88, he was appointed Charles Eliot Norton Professor of Poetry at Harvard University.

John Hollander is A. Bartlett Giamatti Professor of English at Yale University. His most recent collection of poetry is *In Time and Place*. His many books of criticism include *The Figure of Echo* and *Vision and Resonance*.

Elliot Krieger is author of *A Marxist Study of Shakespeare's Comedies*.

Ruth Nevo is Professor of English at Hebrew University at Jerusalem. She is the author of *The Dial of Virtue: A Study of Poems on Affairs of State in the Seventeenth Century, Comic Transformations in Shakespeare*, and *Tragic Form in Shakespeare*. She has also translated into English the *Selected Poems of Chaim Nachman Bialik*.

Coppélia Kahn is Associate Professor of English at Wesleyan University and author of *Man's Estate: Masculine Identity in Shakespeare*. She has also published several articles on Shakespeare.

Karen Greif received her Ph.D. in English from Harvard University in 1982.

Camille Slights lives in Saskatoon, Saskatchewan.

Elizabeth M. Yearling is Lecturer in English at the University of Glasgow in Scotland.

JEAN E. HOWARD is Associate Professor of English at Syracuse University in New York.

GARY TAYLOR is the editor of The Oxford Shakespeare edition of *Henry V* and the co-editor of *The Division of the Kingdoms: Shakespeare's Two Versions of* King Lear. He has written, with Stanley Wells, *Modernizing Shakespeare's Spelling, with Three Studies in the Text of* Henry V.

GEOFFREY H. HARTMAN is Karl Young Professor of English and Comparative Literature at Yale University. His many books include *Wordsworth's Poetry* and *Saving the Text*, a study of Jacques Derrida.

Bibliography

Adams, Barry B. "Orsino and the Spirit of Love: Text, Syntax and Sense in *Twelfth Night* 1.1.1–15." *Shakespeare Quarterly* 29 (1978): 52–59.

Barber, C. L. *Shakespeare's Festive Comedy: A Study of Dramatic Form and Its Relation to Social Custom*. Princeton: Princeton University Press, 1959.

Barton, Anne. "*As You Like It* and *Twelfth Night*: Shakespeare's Sense of an Ending." In *Shakespearean Comedy*, edited by Malcolm Bradbury and David Palmer. Stratford-upon-Avon Studies 14. London: Edward Arnold, 1972.

Bellringer, Alan W. "*Twelfth Night* or *What You Will*: Alternatives." *Durham University Journal* 74 (December 1981): 1–13.

Berry, Ralph. "The Season of *Twelfth Night*." *New York Literary Forum* 1 (1978): 139–49.

———. "*Twelfth Night*: The Experience of the Audience." *Shakespeare Survey* 34 (1981): 121–30.

Bradbrook, M. C. *The Growth and Structure of Elizabethan Comedy*. London: Chatto & Windus, 1962.

Bradley, A. C. "Feste the Jester." In *A Miscellany*, 2d ed. London: Macmillan, 1931.

Braude, Sandra. "Harmony in Illyria: Study of the Twin Themes of Love and Music in Shakespeare's *Twelfth Night*." *Crux* 17 (February 1983): 29–35.

Campbell, Oscar James. *Shakespeare's Satire*. 1943. Reprint. Hamden, Conn.: Archon Books, 1963.

Carroll, William C. "The Ending of *Twelfth Night* and the Tradition of Metamorphosis." *New York Literary Forum* 5–6 (1980): 49–61.

Cave, T. C. "Recognition and the Reader." *Comparative Criticism* 2: (1980) 49–69.

Charney, Maurice. "Comic Premises of *Twelfth Night*." *New York Literary Forum* 1 (1978): 151–65.

———. "*Twelfth Night* and the 'Natural Perspective' of Comedy." In *De Shakespeare à T. S. Eliot: mélanges offerts à Henri Fluchere*, edited by Marie-Jeanne Durry et al., 43–51. Paris: Didier, 1976.

Crane, Milton. "*Twelfth Night* and Shakespearian Comedy." *Shakespeare Quarterly* 6 (1955): 1–8.

Eagleton, Terence. "Language and Reality in *Twelfth Night*." *Critical Quarterly* 9 (1967): 217–28.

Evans, Bertrand. *Shakespeare's Comedies*. Oxford: Clarendon, 1960.

Fortin, René. "*Twelfth Night:* Shakespeare's Drama of Initiation." *Papers on Language and Literature* 8 (Spring 1972): 135–46.

Frye, Northrop. *A Natural Perspective.* New York: Columbia University Press, 1965.

Gregson, J. M. *Shakespeare:* Twelfth Night. London: Edward Arnold, 1980.

Hansen, Niels. "The Comedy of Language and the Language of Comedy." In *Essays Presented to Knud Schibsbye,* edited by Michael Chesnutt et al., 160–63. Copenhagen: University of Copenhagen, 1980.

Harbage, Alfred. *Shakespeare and the Rival Tradition.* Bloomington: Indiana University Press, 1970.

Hassel, R. Chris, Jr. "'Man's Estate': The Festival of Folly in *Twelfth Night.*" In *Faith and Folly in Shakespeare's Romantic Comedies,* 149–75. Athens: University of Georgia Press, 1980.

Hayles, Nancy K. "Sexual Disguises in *As You Like It* and *Twelfth Night.*" *Shakespeare Survey* 32 (1979): 63–72.

Holland, Norman. *The Shakespearean Imagination.* New York: Macmillan, 1964.

Hollander, John. "*Twelfth Night* and the Morality of Indulgence." *Sewanee Review* 67 (1959): 220–38.

Hotson, Leslie. *The First Night of* Twelfth Night. New York: Macmillan, 1954.

Huston, J. Dennis. "'When I Came to Man's Estate': *Twelfth Night* and Problems of Identity." *Modern Language Quarterly* 33 (1972): 274–88.

Kelly, T. J. "*Twelfth Night.*" *Critical Review* 19 (1977): 54–70.

King, Walter, ed. *Twentieth-Century Interpretations of* Twelfth Night: *A Collection of Critical Essays.* Englewood Cliffs, N.J.: Prentice-Hall, 1968.

Kott, Jan. *Shakespeare Our Contemporary.* Translated by Boleslaw Taborski. New York: Norton, 1974.

Leech, Clifford. Twelfth Night *and Shakespearean Comedy.* Toronto: University of Toronto Press, 1965.

Leggatt, Alexander. *Shakespeare's Comedy of Love.* London: Methuen, 1974.

Levin, Harry. "The Underplot of *Twelfth Night.*" In *De Shakespeare à T. S. Eliot: mélanges offerts à Henri Fluchere,* edited by Marie-Jeanne Durry et al., 53–59. Paris: Didier, 1976.

Levin, Richard A. "*Twelfth Night, The Merchant of Venice* and Two Alternate Approaches to Shakespearean Comedy." *English Studies* 59 (1978): 336–43.

Lewalski, Barbara K. "Thematic Patterns in *Twelfth Night.*" In *Shakespeare Studies,* edited by J. Leeds Barroll, 168–79. Cincinnati: University of Cincinnati Press, 1965.

Logan, Thad Jenkins. "*Twelfth Night:* The Limits of Festivity." *Studies in English Literature* 22 (1982): 223–36.

McCary, W. Thomas. *Friends and Lovers: The Phenomenology of Desire in Shakespearean Comedy.* New York: Columbia University Press, 1985.

Mahood, M. M. *Shakespeare's Wordplay.* London: Methuen, 1957.

Mueschke, Pau, and Jeannette Fleisher. "Jonsonian Elements in the Comic Underplot of *Twelfth Night.*" *PMLA* 48 (1933): 720–40.

Muir, Kenneth, ed. *Shakespeare: The Comedies.* Englewood Cliffs, N.J.: Prentice-Hall, 1965.

Murry, John Middleton. *Shakespeare.* London: J. Cape, 1936.

Nagarajan, S. "*What You Will:* A Suggestion." *Shakespearian Quarterly* 10 (1959): 61–67.

Palmer, D., and M. Bradbury, eds. *Shakespearean Comedy*. London: Edward Arnold, 1972.

Palmer, D. J. Twelfth Night: *A Casebook*. New York: Macmillan, 1972.

———. "*Twelfth Night* and the Myth of Echo and Narcissus." *Shakespeare Survey* 32 (1979): 73–77.

Phialas, Peter. *Shakespeare's Romantic Comedies: The Development of Their Form and Meaning*. Chapel Hill: University of North Carolina Press, 1966.

Rose, Mark. *Shakespearean Design*. Cambridge: Belknap Press of Harvard University Press, 1972.

Salingar, Leo. "The Design of *Twelfth Night*." *Shakespeare Quarterly* 9 (Spring 1958): 117–39.

———. *Shakespeare and the Traditions of Comedy*. Cambridge: Cambridge University Press, 1974.

Schucking, Levin L. *Character Problems in Shakespeare's Plays*. London: G. G. Harrap, 1922.

Siegel, Paul N. "Malvolio: Comic Puritan Automaton." *New York Literary Forum* 5–6 (1980): 217–30.

Stoll, E. E. *Shakespeare and Other Masters*. Cambridge: Harvard University Press, 1940.

Styan, J. I. *The Shakespeare Revolution: Criticism and Performance in the Twentieth Century*. Cambridge: Cambridge University Press, 1977.

Summers, Joseph H. "The Masks of *Twelfth Night*." *Kansas City Review* 22 (October 1955): 25–32.

Swinden, Patrick. *An Introduction to Shakespeare's Comedies*. London: Macmillan, 1973.

Tilley, M. P. "The Organic Unity of *Twelfth Night*." *PMLA* 29 (1914): 550–66.

———. "Shakespeare and his Ridicule of *Cambyses*." *MLN* 24 (1909): 244–47.

Ungerer, Gustav. " 'My Lady's a Catayan, We are Politicians, Malvolio's a Peg-a-ramsie.' " *Shakespeare Survey* 32 (1979): 85–104.

———. "Sir Andrew Aguecheek and His Head of Hair." *Shakespeare Studies* 16 (1983): 101–33.

Warren, Roger. " 'Smiling at Grief': Some Techniques of Comedy in *Twelfth Night* and *Cosi Fan Tutte*." *Shakespeare Survey* 32 (1979): 79–84.

Welsford, Enid. *The Fool: His Social and Literary History*. London: Faber & Faber, 1935. Reprint. New York: Doubleday, 1961.

Willbern, David. "Malvolio's Fall." *Shakespeare Quarterly* 29 (1978): 85–90.

Williams, Charles. "The Use of the Second Person in *Twelfth Night*. *English* 9 (Spring 1953): 125–28.

Williams, Porter, Jr. "Mistakes in *Twelfth Night* and Their Resolution." *PMLA* 76 (1961): 193–99.

Wilson, John Dover. *Shakespeare's Happy Comedies*. Evanston, Ill.: Northwestern University Press, 1962.

Woodbridge, Linda. " 'Fire in Your Heart and Brimstone in Your Liver': Towards an Unsaturnalian *Twelfth Night*." *The Southern Review* 17 (1984): 270–91.

Acknowledgments

"Shakespeare's Many Sorts of Music" (originally entitled " 'The Diapason Closing Full in Man': The Musical Subjects in Humanist Poetry") by John Hollander from *The Untuning of the Sky: Ideas of Music in English Poetry 1500–1700* by John Hollander, © 1961 by John Hollander. Reprinted by permission of Princeton University Press and the author.

"Malvolio and Class Ideology in *Twelfth Night*" (originally entitled *"Twelfth Night"*) by Elliot Krieger from *A Marxist Study of Shakespeare's Comedies* by Elliot Krieger, © 1979 by Elliot Krieger. Reprinted by permission of Macmillan, London and Basingstoke, and Barnes & Noble Books, Totowa, New Jersey.

"Nature's Bias" by Ruth Nevo from *Comic Transformation in Shakespeare* by Ruth Nevo, © 1980 by Ruth Nevo. Reprinted by permission of Methuen & Co. Ltd.

"Choosing the Right Mate in *Twelfth Night*" (originally entitled "The Providential Tempest") by Coppélia Kahn from *Man's Estate: Masculine Identity in Shakespeare* by Coppélia Kahn, © 1981 by the Regents of the University of California. Reprinted by permission of the University of California Press.

"Plays and Playing in *Twelfth Night*" by Karen Greif from *Shakespeare Survey: An Annual Survey of Shakespearean Study and Production* 34, edited by Stanley Wells, © 1981 by Cambridge University Press. Reprinted by permission of Cambridge University Press.

"The Principle of Recompense in *Twelfth Night*" by Camille Slights from *Modern Language Review* 77, no. 3 (July 1982), © 1982 by the Modern Humanities Research Association. Reprinted by permission of the Modern Humanities Research Association.

"Language, Theme, and Character in *Twelfth Night*" by Elizabeth M. Yearling from *Shakespeare Survey: An Annual Survey of Shakespearean Study and Production* 35, edited by Stanley Wells, © 1982 by the Estate of Elizabeth Yearling. Reprinted by permission of Cambridge University Press.

"The Orchestration of *Twelfth Night:* The Rhythm of Restraint and Release" by Jean E. Howard from *Shakespeare's Art of Orchestration: Stage Technique and Audience Response* by Jean E. Howard, © 1984 by the Board of Trustees of the University of Illinois. Reprinted by permission of the University of Illinois Press.

"Shakespeare's Realism: Viola" (originally entitled "Who is Viola? What is She?") by Gary Taylor from *To Analyze Delight: A Hedonist Criticism of Shakespeare* by Gary Taylor, © 1985 by Gary Taylor. Reprinted by permission.

"Shakespeare's Poetical Character in *Twelfth Night*" by Geoffrey H. Hartman from *Shakespeare and the Question of Theory*, edited by Patricia Parker and Geoffrey H. Hartman, © 1985 by Geoffrey H. Hartman. Reprinted by permission.

Index